T0324294

Aggression in Play Therapy

A Norton Professional Book

Aggression in Play Therapy

A Neurobiological Approach for Integrating Intensity

LISA DION

FOREWORD BY BONNIE BADENOCH

W. W. NORTON & COMPANY | NEW YORK · LONDON

Independent Publishers Since 1923

For information about permission to reproduce selections from this book, write to Permissions, W. W. Norton & Company, Inc., 500 Fifth Avenue, New York, NY 10110

For information about special discounts for bulk purchases, please contact W. W. Norton Special Sales at specialsales@wwnorton.com or 800-233-4830

Manufacturing by LSC Harrisonburg
Production manager: Katelyn MacKenzie

Library of Congress Cataloging-in-Publication Data
Names: Dion, Lisa (Play therapist), author.
Title: Aggression in play therapy : a neurobiological approach
for integrating intensity / Lisa Dion.
Description: First edition. | New York : W.W. Norton & Company, [2018] |
"A Norton Professional Book." | Includes bibliographical references and index.
Identifiers: LCCN 2018016669 | ISBN 9780393713190 (hardcover)
Subjects: LCSH: Play therapy. | Psychic trauma in children—Treatment. |
Psychotherapist and patient.
Classification: LCC RJ505.P6 D55 2018 | DDC 618.92/891653—dc23
LC record available at https://lccn.loc.gov/2018016669

W. W. Norton & Company, Inc., 500 Fifth Avenue, New York, N.Y. 10110
www.wwnorton.com

W. W. Norton & Company Ltd., 15 Carlisle Street, London W1D 3BS

4 5 6 7 8 9 0

CONTENTS

*This book is dedicated to all my child clients,
my students, and my own daughter, Avery,
for teaching me that the best way to navigate
challenging situations is to be yourself
and take deep breaths*

FOREWORD

Today, as never before, we are aware of both the fragility and resilience of our children. Relational neuroscience has illuminated the ways in which their still-developing embodied brains respond to overwhelming experiences of pain and fear, storing them away to be healed when the necessary interpersonal conditions arrive. Until that help comes, memory of these traumatic events shapes their thoughts, feelings, behaviors, and relationships in ways that often understandably stir up fear, confusion, and sometimes reprisals in the adults around them. This is particularly true if the way the child adapts and expresses his or her distress is through anger and aggression.

How, then, can there be help for these children? Two years ago, when I first met Lisa, it was clear that she had a different understanding of the value of aggression than most of our culture. Instead of seeing it as bad behavior in need of correction, she understood it to be the child's necessary adaptive strategy in the face of unmanageable experiences of fear and pain. There is something quite beautiful and potentially healing in placing anger and aggression on the list of legitimate ways in which we express our distress and protect ourselves. Affective neuroscientist Jaak Panksepp (Panksepp & Bivens, 2012) would agree. He tells us that at the roots of our emotional life lies RAGE, one of the seven emotional-motivational systems that is particularly aroused when we feel alone with grief and fear. It is often the final cry for help before we collapse into immobility. It is equally a powerful communication about the depth of pain and fear we have endured.

When Lisa suggests that we see beyond the behavior to the child inside the actions, and that we "be with" rather than try to change or fix what the child is doing, she is reaching right down to the roots of how welcoming and working with aggression can be a doorway to healing trauma in play therapy. In fact, to close off the exploration of aggression is to leave parts of the trauma unseen and unintegrated. Grounding her work in the wisdom of Stephen Porges's Polyvagal Theory, she offers a pathway toward regulating and integrating these highly aroused states within the embrace of the therapeutic relationship.

This becomes the second and equally important focus of her book. How do we therapists prepare ourselves to be with aggression so we can hold whatever our children bring into the room? Lisa answers this with abundant wise and empathic support for play therapists. She never underestimates the challenge of being with such charged emotions and highly energized behaviors, recognizing that our own history of being exposed to aggression or being aggressive ourselves is bound to be touched and awakened. Instead, she offers mindfulness, breath, movement, and naming our internal state to cultivate the necessary inner awareness and expansion of our window of tolerance that can allow us to become the external co-regulators with our young ones. Combining stabilizing information about how our autonomic nervous system responds to trauma and interpersonal connection, and how traumatic memories can be integrated (food for our left hemispheres) with stories, reflections, and practices (nourishment for our right hemispheres), she marks out a clear pathway for gradually increasing our ability to be a reliable resource for our children.

Building on this foundation, she weaves together many skills that provide reassuring specifics on which to rely in this challenging work. The practice of speaking our authentic truth about what we are experiencing either as part of or observer of the play ("I'm scared." "I don't understand why they are fighting.") while also remembering that it is just play is central. This lies at the heart of her understanding of the power of resonance to let children know they are being heard accurately and also to model regulation of these states. As we therapists are able to hold our own activations in the broad embrace of our window of tolerance, our little ones will learn to do the same. She speaks about boundaries as primarily for the benefit of the therapist who is about to be overwhelmed, about the ongoing cycle of rupture and repair to relieve us of the burden of perfection, and about death play as an essential skill to heal the hypo-aroused nervous system. But most of all, she speaks about her faith in the power of the dyad to craft a healing space together. This book is full of the wisdom, hope, support, and accompaniment—the essentials we all need as we offer ourselves to these most vulnerable and resilient young beings.

Bonnie Badenoch
Vancouver, Washington
July 1, 2018

Aggression in Play Therapy

INTRODUCTION

IN 2002, I WALKED INTO MY FIRST PLAYROOM AS A play therapist. I was excited and terrified simultaneously. Like many play therapists when they first begin, I didn't have a lot of training. I was in my internship, venturing into the world of working with children therapeutically for the first time. I didn't really know what to do other than play and try to connect with the 9-year-old boy who was waiting for me to somehow help him transform his pain. Somehow I was supposed to know how to do that.

As I worked with more and more children, I dedicated myself to learning as many play therapy theories and models that I could. I read books. I attended conferences. I participated in weeklong intensive trainings. I wanted to understand how to work with children, but in everything I studied, something for me still felt missing. As I studied, I found myself searching for why and how play therapy works. I felt that with this understanding, I could support a deeper level of healing with my child clients.

My career as a play therapist took me on a journey working in adoption agencies, foster care homes, social service treatment teams, school counseling rooms, orphanages, hospital settings, and my own play therapy office. It didn't matter where I went; children with trauma found me. This meant that children struggling with aggression found me, or maybe we found each other.

This book addresses one of the biggest issues that every play therapist experiences but often wants to avoid: aggression. Aggression can be so scary and overwhelming that sometimes we want to stick our heads in the sand and pretend that it doesn't actually exist. At a minimum, we sometimes just want to make it stop and go away. We have become so frightened by aggression that when it shows up, our first impulse is typically to shut it down.

I would like to tell you that I went to a training and learned exactly what to do when aggression entered the play-room so that I could support these children, but I didn't. At the time, very few trainings and writings were in the field geared specifically toward working with aggression. It was the children and my intuition that taught me.

We live in a culture that teaches children that aggression is wrong. So much of the education on aggression that children receive at school and in their homes is behavior based. In my opinion, we are missing the child inside the behavior. The biggest lesson that children have taught me over the years is to look beyond their behaviors in order to see them. They have taught me that their aggression is an extension of the fear and dysregulation that lives inside of them, driven by their perceptions of themselves and of the world around them. They have taught me how to "be with them" instead of trying to "do something to them" in order to help them transform.

As the fields of neuroscience and interpersonal neurobiology have emerged, the findings have given language to what my clients have been attempting to teach me over the years and what I was intuiting in the playroom—that therapists being their authentic selves, coupled with not being afraid to move toward the aggression and become the external regulator, was one of the key elements in transforming aggression. When we start to move beyond behavior modification into an understanding of what is happening in the brains and bodies of our clients, a whole new possibility for integration opens up.

For the first time in history, we have the research and an understanding of what is happening inside the client, inside the therapist, and between client and therapist to guide us deeper into the relationship so that we can begin to work with aggression and integrate intensity in ways that allow for a deeper transformation.

This book is the resource I wish I'd had on my shelf sixteen years ago.

Parts of this book are found in my first, self-published book, *Integrating Extremes: Aggression and Death in the Playroom*. The book you now have in your hands is an updated, transformed version of that book, filled with more stories, more insight, and more neuroscience.

As you read this book, you will discover that it is just

as much for you as it is for your child clients. Aggression affects both the therapist and the client in the playroom. A book filled only with techniques and ideas on how to help children decrease their aggression would miss one of the most important parts of the equation: you. Play therapists are on the front line every day with children, feeling the intensity of the children's play and stories. As such, play therapists are highly susceptible to burnout and compassion fatigue. This book will address how to help children integrate their aggression, as well as show therapists how to work in such a way that supports their own health and nervous system regulation.

It was my goal to write a book that offers knowledge as well as inspires you to embrace yourself fully in the playroom. I have witnessed time and again the magic that occurs when therapists allow themselves to fully show up, while modeling self-regulation and a deep connection to self. I believe that it is the moments when we transcend our "shoulds" that we allow ourselves to be guided by a deeper wisdom.

As you move away and avoid your emotions and sensations, you will lose yourself and your center. I want to give you permission to move toward anger, aggression, and other intense emotions. Embrace them. Learn how to dance with them so that you can transform their energy and let it lead to new possibilities for yourself and your clients. Transcend your limiting beliefs regarding aggression so that you can awaken your certainty and presence.

It is in this space that deep healing has a chance to occur for our clients and for ourselves. I hope that this book provides you with tools to help you navigate aggressive play. And I hope that somewhere in this book you find hope and new possibility.

I also want to remind you to be kind to yourself on this journey. You are the most important toy in the playroom.

Aggression in the Playroom

THE SWORDS WERE FLYING. I WAS DODGING AND blocking the blows, but I was barely able to keep up with this 5-year-old's swings. I was beginning to feel overwhelmed. In this whirlwind of energy, all my brain was registering was "Protect myself, protect myself, protect myself." Seconds later, I felt something hard hit my head. The pain brought me back to the moment, and I immediately knew it wasn't the sword he was using. Without the ability to block out an authentic response, I sank to the floor with tears welling in my eyes and blurted out, "I'm scared." This little boy, who was a witness and victim of domestic violence, looked into my eyes, put down his weapons and crawled into my lap. He began to gently rock back and forth, saying, "Me, too. Me, too." In that moment, I finally understood his world. I felt it at my core.

In my session with Carlos, when the sense of overwhelm got to be too much, I lost my ability to stay present. I emotionally flooded and checked out. It was the blow to my head that brought me back. The shock and pain was so intense that I wasn't able to block out my authentic response, and when Carlos saw me sink to the floor with tears in my eyes, he knew that I was being real and that I understood his fear. In fact, that moment changed the course of our therapy together. His trauma play integrated and diminished significantly, and the relationship between us deepened to a level that I had not been expecting. The experience also led me into a deep inquiry regarding aggressive play, boundaries, and therapist self-care.

Through my roles as a supervisor and teacher, I've heard hundreds of therapists' stories about their confusion and emotional struggles regarding aggressive play. They've also told me about the physical pain they've endured trying to help some of their child clients. I've heard stories of sessions filled with play containing sword fights, being killed and left to die, being handcuffed and locked away, explosions, dismemberment, injured babies, sexual intrusion, and physical abuse. Whenever I teach workshops on this topic, I ask participants to raise their hands if they have ever been hurt or thought they were going to get hurt in a play therapy session. Each time, over 90% of the audience raises their hands. I've listened to therapists questioning their role in the playroom, whether or not they want to be play therapists, and, more importantly, questioning themselves. I get it. I've struggled with these dilemmas, too.

When I first became a play therapist, I discovered that

I had the capacity to work with high levels of trauma with both nondirective and directive approaches, but no one taught me how to avoid absorbing the high level of intense energy that comes from being a part of or witnessing this type of play. After sessions, I often felt drained, tired, and agitated. But I also saw that the children I was working with were transforming and becoming empowered. Their play was integrating and their symptoms were diminishing. I wanted to help them heal, but I didn't want to be a punching bag or a trauma trash can. Whether I was watching a child play aggressively or I was experiencing the aggression directly, the energy was so jarring to my nervous system that I knew I had to change something or I'd be at major risk for compassion fatigue, burnout, or injury.

Moments of truth, like the one that came when I was hit on the head while playing with Carlos, together with the messages I received from listening to my body, inspired my journey to discover how to help children heal by using methods that support them and myself as their therapist. Thanks to the thousands of children I've worked with directly and indirectly and the therapists who have so courageously shared their struggles with me, I have a new perspective on aggressive play, which I'll share with you throughout this book.

A PROMISING NEW PARADIGM

Aggression in Play Therapy introduces a perspective of aggression from the understanding of the nervous system and interpersonal neurobiology. When we look at aggression from this perspective, we begin to understand that children's biology is attempting to integrate their sympathetic (hyper-aroused) and dorsal parasympathetic (hypo-aroused) states as they work through their traumatic memories and sensations. It also begins to help us understand the role of the therapist in supporting regulation and helping repattern a child's nervous system, while promoting integration. Both of these are necessary components in making aggressive play therapeutic, which will be discussed throughout this book.

This book is for mental health professionals who work with children between the ages of 3 and 12 whose play displays a high level of intensity and aggression. Navigating sword fights, being handcuffed and shot, and watching violent play while staying present and facilitating the intensity is not easy to do. Often, we're taken right to the edge of our capacity to hold the energy in the playroom, and we lose ourselves for a moment (or longer). This book presents a paradigm that's a way back to yourself so that you can help children heal at profound levels and access the most authentic parts of yourself in the process. It's the art of learning how to be authentic in the playroom while facilitating a deep level of healing for the child. Although this book focuses on the intensity that arises with aggression in the playroom, all children's biology is attempting to integrate their hyper- and hypo-aroused states as they play out their perceptions. So what you learn in this book will help you with all your clients, not just the challenging ones.

Most of us decided to become play therapists because we have a sincere desire to help children. We're led by a yearning to help children heal. We didn't choose this profession to get physically or emotional hurt, but sometimes we do. The new paradigm I'm presenting is a framework for helping us to authentically work with the intensity of aggressive play without getting hurt or causing our nervous systems to start shutting down in response to the intensity, which is the first step in helping to integrate aggression.

What you will learn is rooted in neuroscience and what is happening in the mind. It is a template to help you understand how to work with the intensity and its impact on your own nervous system, as well as a guide to help you understand how to make aggressive play therapeutic. It is not an exact recipe, as you will soon learn. It is up to you to be attuned to what is needed in any given moment in the playroom.

KNOW THE BASICS

This book acknowledges and respects the therapeutic benefits and powers of play. Play fosters emotional wellness, facilitates communication, increases personal strengths, and enhances social relationships in children (Schaeffer & Drewes, 2012). Play therapy has been well established as a developmentally appropriate therapeutic intervention for children (Bratton & Ray, 2000; Bratton, Ray, Rhide, & Jones, 2005).

The information in this book also isn't a substitute for

basic play therapy skills. The information is an addition to what you already know how to do in the playroom. Some readers may be trained in a more nondirective approach, while others might be trained in a more directive approach. Whether you choose to be more nondirective or directive is up to you. Overall, I tend to be more nondirective, becoming more directive as more containment is needed or if the children's play requires a more directive intervention to support their healing. The examples in this book are more nondirective in nature, but all of the information presented can easily be integrated into a more directive approach. It is my belief that knowing both is important, as not every model fits every child, and different approaches are needed at different times in a child's process.

SOMETIMES PLAY THERAPY ISN'T ENOUGH

In the cases of most of the children you work with, you'll be able to add the framework I am going to teach you to your current training to help them integrate their traumatic experiences while keeping yourself safe and minimizing signs of compassion fatigue in your own nervous system. In other cases, it will be a piece of the puzzle. It is important to acknowledge that each child needs something different, and sometimes play therapy alone isn't enough for some children. Children who have experienced highly traumatic events often need additional support such as occupational therapy, speech therapy, academic support, or intensive family play therapy. The caregivers of these children often need intensive parenting support. Whenever possible, make sure you're working with the family and caregivers to give them the tools and supports they need, because they also need our help along this journey. Use your best clinical judgment to know when you need to bring in additional help and support. The last thing I will say is that it is important that you are not doing this work alone. Seek out supervision and peer support to help you process what you are experiencing in sessions. This work is not easy work.

SYNERGETIC PLAY THERAPY

The foundation for the paradigm I'm presenting is influenced by Synergetic Play Therapy—a model I created and teach. I draw from my own stories in the playroom and from some of the principles of this model to help us explore what's happening between the therapist and the child during aggressive play. You don't need to be a Synergetic Play Therapist or to have studied this model of play therapy to understand the concepts in this book. Synergetic Play Therapy combines the therapeutic powers of play with nervous system regulation, interpersonal neurobiology, physics, attachment theory, mindfulness, and therapist authenticity. Its primary play therapy influences are Child-Centered, Experiential, and Gestalt theories.

Although Synergetic Play Therapy is a model of play therapy, it's often also referred to as a way of being in relationship with self and other. The model's philosophy is an all-encompassing paradigm that can be applied to any facet of life; and subsequently, any model of play therapy can be applied to it, or vice versa. As a model, Synergetic Play Therapy is both nondirective and directive in its application. Use the information in this book to deepen whatever type of play therapy you do. The information will help you develop a greater understanding of yourself in the playroom and will show you how to facilitate aggressive play in a way that truly allows healing to occur for the child and for you. (Visit synergeticplaytherapy.com for more information on this model.)

PLAYING WITH INTENSITY

As therapists, we're asked to engage in aggressive play in two primary ways. One is dramatic play that we're actively participating in. It might involve a sword fight, a gunfight, being handcuffed and arrested, being injured, or being killed. The other way is when we're in the role of the observer. In this play, we watch as the child wages a massive war in the sand tray, creates intense images through art, stacks blocks and kicks them down, makes stuffed toys pummel each other, or leaves wounded dolls alone and neglected. Whether we're participating in or watching this type of play, it's intense because it activates both the sympathetic (hyper-aroused) and dorsal parasympathetic (hypo-aroused) states of our nervous system. Both extremes are uncomfortable, so our gut reaction is often to avoid them.

It's normal for therapists to be somewhat uncomfortable with extreme energy, especially if we don't know what to do with it or what it means. Let's be honest—it can be scary! If we have negative associations in our personal history that remotely resemble or remind us of that energy, it's even scarier, and our protective patterns will probably come into play. This is normal and will happen. Facilitating aggressive play isn't about avoiding or trying to prevent the intensity from happening—it's about learning how to be with yourself and your experience so that you can move toward what you're experiencing, which creates the opportunity to change your own neural wiring and protective patterns. Once you learn how to stay connected to yourself in the midst of the fear, you can manage and integrate what you're experiencing. This book will teach you how to do this so that you can teach your clients how to do the same.

In my opinion, many play therapists are not well educated in how to make aggressive play therapeutic, as much of what therapists are taught is how to stop or control the aggression. It is also my opinion that many play therapists don't understand how to manage the intensity in their own bodies so that they don't develop signs of compassion fatigue or burnout. These opinions come from my observations over the years in this field while supervising and training therapists in private practice settings, agency settings, social service departments, hospitals, and schools both nationally and internationally. I've observed the impact this has had on therapists, including myself. Since we're not superhuman, high levels of intensity can affect our lives outside of the playroom. Before I had an understanding of neurobiology and how the mind works, or knew how to use regulation in a therapy session, I had many sessions where I walked out at the end thinking, "I just got emotionally beat up for 45 minutes!" or it all just felt like "too much." At times, I even took it personally and felt angry with the child. Often my agitation would spill over into other areas of my life, leaving me and my loved ones feeling frustrated and overwhelmed.

I realized that we have to work with our experience or we'll spend our time shut down or overwhelmed, putting ourselves at risk for burnout and compassion fatigue. We might start having nightmares, snap at our loved ones, or find it difficult not to think about our clients when we aren't at the office. Another common reaction is to become desensitized or emotionally numb. We might experience signs or symptoms of depression or become very analytical, obsessively trying to figure out what happened to certain kids to distract ourselves from what we're feeling. These are all symptoms of a dysregulated nervous system, meaning that our nervous system is feeling out of whack as a result of our own perceptions and our lack of regulation.

YOU ARE NOT ALONE

If you've felt overwhelmed, shut down, physically exhausted, sleep-deprived, and dreaded seeing certain clients, you're not alone. Have you ever looked at your schedule and thought, "Oh no! I have to see Johnny at 4:00," as you feel the intensity or exhaustion of the last session creep into your body? If so, you know what I'm talking about. I want you to know that this is all common and normal. I have yet to meet a play therapist who didn't struggle with this at some point. The reason these symptoms are normal is that our brains are wired to perceive aggression as a potential threat because instinctually we know we might not be safe. It's no wonder, then, that we cringe a little when a client starts racing around the room shooting us, throwing toys at us, leaving us to die, or creating aggressive play for us to observe.

IT STARTS WITH YOU

Integrating intensity and making aggressive play therapeutic starts with you, the therapist. I am going to emphasize this throughout this book. This may be a paradigm shift if you've learned that your only job is to hold space for the client and keep your own experience at bay. I am going to use research and neuroscience to show you why you are one of the key components in making aggressive play therapeutic. As such, the chapters ahead are going to teach you how to manage what is happening inside of you during your sessions, while showing you what to do when aggression shows up in the playroom. Get ready to go on a personal journey as you delve into this book.

CHOOSING TOYS FOR TRAUMA WORK

Over the years, I've seen a wide range of aggressive toys in the playroom: plastic knives, handcuffs, bop bags, all types of swords, and everything from three-inch water guns to plastic machine guns that look and sound real. But I haven't seen a correlation between what the toys look like and the depth that children will go to in their work with toys. I've seen kids resist going deeper for other reasons, but it's never been about the toys themselves.

Children will use whatever is available to do their work. I suggest that therapists have aggressive toys to help kids work through their traumatic memories and emotions, but I don't think the toys have to look real. For example, children will use a three-inch fluorescent water gun the same way they'll use a toy that looks like a real machine gun. (For the water gun, make sure to fill the hole with Play-Doh and take out the stopper unless you really want it to be used as a water gun!) Using toys that don't look like real weapons helps to keep the aggression inside the playroom, because the emphasis is on facilitation and integration of the aggressive energy, as opposed to shooting the therapist with a gun that looks real.

When you're thinking about which toys to have in your playroom, consider ones that do the job but don't necessarily resemble the real thing. For example, I've discovered that the best sword is a pool noodle cut in half to make a pair. They're cheap, they don't bend like most play swords, and they don't hurt when they hit you. Set the pool-noodle swords next to a shield and children will know exactly what to do with them. Since they don't look like swords, they can also be used in other ways.

Carefully considering the types of aggressive toys you have in the playroom will also help you to work more effectively with the children's parents and caregivers. Most parents, at one point or another, will see the playroom, and parents who are uncomfortable with aggression will express fear or nonacceptance of the aggressive toys you have. Toys that look less threatening promote the healing without triggering the parents' fear response. If you have parents who express concern about the aggressive toys, you have the option to take those toys out. Children will do their work regardless of whether a particular toy is available or not. If they need to work on aggression, they'll turn a marker into a knife, make a gun out of Legos, or use their forefinger and thumb to shoot you. You can also choose to educate the parents on the importance of aggressive play in the play therapy process.

Now that we've covered some basics, grab your swords, shields, and helmets as we jump into exploring aggression in the playroom.

CHAPTER 1 KEY POINTS

- Understanding aggression in play therapy from a nervous system and interpersonal neurobiology perspective helps you understand your role and how to make it therapeutic.

- *Aggression in Play Therapy* is a resource to be used in addition to the basic Play Therapy skills you've already learned.

- The information contained in this book is based on neuroscience, interpersonal neurobiology, and principles from Synergetic Play Therapy. All of the information can be applied to both directive and nondirective approaches in play therapy.

- Making aggressive play therapeutic starts with you! And you cannot do the work alone. Supervision and support are crucial.

- It is important to choose aggressive toys that do the job but don't necessarily look like the real thing. This helps to not promote the aggression outside of the playroom.

Exploring a New Perspective: Embracing Aggression

AGGRESSION IS A SYMPTOM OF SYMPATHETIC NER-vous system activation when a child is perceiving a threat or challenge. Oxford Dictionaries defines aggression as "hostile or violent behaviour" or attitudes toward another with a "readiness to attack or confront." It is a normal biological response that arises when our sense of safety or our ideas about who we think we are, who others are supposed to be, and how we think the world is supposed to operate are compromised. Aggression can be expressed outwardly, such as in hitting, biting, kicking, and yelling, or it can be expressed inwardly, resulting in self-harming behaviors.

This book focuses on aggression that emerges through the child's play in a play therapy session.

THE PLAYROOM IS THE PERFECT PLACE FOR AGGRESSION

When children start to play aggressively in a session, we can get caught up in trying to decide if we should let it go on or stop it. "Is this OK?" "Should I allow this?" "If we play like this, are they going to play like this with their friends?" "Am I promoting aggression?" "Am I replaying the trauma?" "Should I be teaching social norms such as hitting is not appropriate?" These are the questions I hear every time I teach a seminar on working with aggression. They speak to the confusion that often arises inside us. Without understanding what the aggression actually means or how to work with it, we often default to what we think is the right thing to do, which may not be the most therapeutic thing.

The playroom is the children's safe and contained place for exploring whatever they need to explore to help them feel better. It's the place where they get to do things, say things, and move in ways that may not be considered acceptable outside the playroom.

When we're supporting children in working through experiences they have perceived as traumatic, we have to be willing to let in any aspect of the trauma that needs to enter the room so that the child can work through it with our help. This includes aggression.

Taking aggression out of the playroom or telling children that their aggression is not OK is potentially shutting down an important aspect of what they need to explore in order to heal. The irony is that if the children are not able to explore the aggressive urges and thoughts inside of them during a play therapy session, they may be forced to continue to express their aggression outside of the playroom in order to explore it. In our attempts to stop it, we may actually be reinforcing it.

For this reason, it is my belief that the playroom is the perfect place for aggression.

Aggression in Play Therapy offers ways to make exploring aggression therapeutic without promoting it outside the playroom. The beautiful thing is that as we help our child clients explore their aggressive urges in ways that promote healing, we're also teaching them how to be in relationship with others.

CATHARSIS

It is important that we differentiate what this book is teaching from catharsis theory. The idea of catharsis dates back to Aristotle, when it was suggested that watching tragic plays was a way for viewers to release their negative emotions. The word *catharsis* means to cleanse or purge. The thought behind catharsis theory is that people build up aggression and pressure inside, and the release of these negative emotions decreases the tension, ultimately leading to less aggression. This idea has led to therapeutic interventions such as punching pillows, throwing things, screaming, and so forth. Much of the research regarding catharsis as a way to decrease aggression shows that venting aggression actually creates more anger and hostility (Bushman, 2002; Geen & Quanty, 1977).

This has important implications for play therapists when aggression shows up in the room. Do we just allow the child to vent? Do we let the child whale on a punching bag? Do we encourage the child to punch a pillow to "get it out"? Do we let the child play aggressively with the toys? The concern, of course, is that if we allow the child to do these things, it will increase the aggression or, at minimum, encourage the child to act out more aggressively outside of the playroom. What this book is proposing is integration, not catharsis. Integration requires mindfulness and regulation while children are exploring their thoughts, feelings, and body sensations.

Before we begin to explore the nervous system and what is happening in the playroom when a child becomes aggressive, we first need to look at the current cultural paradigm.

NOT SAYING NO TO AGGRESSION

Let's examine a common situation experienced by most children. Imagine Dave, age 4, is outside on the playground of his preschool. He is playing with his most favorite toy—the truck. This isn't just any truck; this truck is a loader. You can put sand in the back and you can dump it out. Dave is completely fascinated by this truck. As Dave is exploring everything this truck can do, another child walks over and takes the truck out of his hands. In an instant, Dave goes from happy-go-lucky to angry. He gets up and goes over to the child who just took his truck and pushes him.

I have presented this scenario in many of my courses and then asked my students to share with me what they feel would happen next. The answers are unanimous. Dave would most likely be approached by a teacher and told to use his words, and that we don't hurt our friends. He might also be removed from the playground.

I am going to ask you to look deeply at this scenario, as this has become the cultural norm for dealing with aggression. When aggression shows up, the answer is to tell a child that it is not OK.

What did Dave learn in this scenario? Are you ready for the truth? Dave potentially learned that when he has an impulse in his body, he should not trust it. He also potentially learned to disconnect from his body in order to follow a set of rules and to be accepted. Dave learned almost nothing about the aggressive urges inside of him other than that they are wrong. Dave didn't learn how to understand what was happening inside of him, how to honor the urges in his body and to redirect their expression.

We are in a culture that repeatedly gives children messages that aggression is not acceptable, and then we wonder why many children grow up to become adults who engage in violence. *What we suppress, we eventually express.* At minimum, children grow up learning not to understand and trust their instincts and impulses, which over time can lead to a disconnected relationship with their bodies. It also leads to feelings of shame and guilt when they do feel angry and aggressive. The challenge with this is that it is in our bodies that we gather all of the information we need to develop empathy, read nonverbal cues from others, and attune to others. It is no wonder that so many adults struggle in relationship.

As therapists, we can apply this same understanding in the playroom. Ending the session or using the word *no* is often used in play therapy when a child becomes aggressive with the therapist or the toys. Of course, there is a time and place for this, as we will explore when we look at boundaries, but the risk of ending sessions and using *no* as the go-to word is that the play is shut down and the children fail to learn about themselves. The children instead stay focused on whether or not their behavior is accepted by the therapist, missing a much deeper therapeutic opportunity. The core questions are: How do we teach children to recognize and manage the aggressive urges in their bodies, without shaming them or promoting disconnection from their experience? How do we turn the aggression into a mindful experience where children can begin to know themselves and transform the aggression, separating it from catharsis? We need to be asking these questions, rather than just focusing on whether the behavior is right or wrong.

Finding ways to help children when they are aggressive without shaming them or shutting down the play is incredibly important. As I noted earlier, the playroom is the perfect place for children to get permission to explore this challenging emotional state in a way that is healing, repatterning, and nonshaming, but it requires therapists to take a look at their own history with aggression and to pay attention to what they do when aggression shows up in the playroom.

SHAME

When children act out or play aggressively, the messages telling them that their behavior is not OK are often internalized. This can lead to internalized shame. For many children, when they look back and realize what happened, who was affected, and what was said, the shame can increase even more. The catch is that in the moment the children became aggressive, they were having a natural reaction in their bodies to the perception of a challenge or threat.

I remember years ago working with a little boy who, when I went to greet him in the waiting room, was sitting away from his mom and didn't look happy. When he stood up and started to walk toward me, his mom shared that he had been kicked out of his classroom that day. My client's head dropped as he heard the disappointment and judgment in his mom's voice. During our session, he played out the scene that had happened earlier at school. The interesting thing about his play was that his emphasis was on the confusion he felt about what he had done. Was he bad? Was he good? He had no idea, and this was what he was trying to sort through.

The shame, guilt, and confusion was palpable in his play

as he tried to process the messages he'd heard from others regarding what had happened. As he played, I acknowledged what he was trying to help me understand. When I said to him, "This is all so confusing. It is hard to know if what happened was good or bad," he looked at me and started to talk about what had happened. He shared with me that the child he hit had bumped into him, and it caught him by surprise. He'd responded by shocking the child back with a hit. In his mind, he'd been following the urge in his body and reacting from fear. He hadn't consciously chosen to hit; he'd responded quickly. He had then been punished.

This client taught me so much about the shame and confusion that children often feel as a result of how the adults in their lives handle the aggression they express. This includes in the playroom, too.

The keys to making aggression therapeutic that we are going to explore are:

1. Therapists must become the external regulators to help modulate the intensity. Children need to be able to borrow the therapist's regulatory capacity.

2. Any intervention must encourage children to become mindful of the thoughts, feelings, and sensations in their bodies.

3. Therapists model to children how to stay connected to themselves in the midst of the intensity so that children can observe and learn alternative ways of working with the intensity.

4. Therapists must be authentic and congruent to promote feelings of safety for children. If not, the children will escalate the play.

5. Boundaries must be set when the aggression moves outside of therapists' windows of tolerance and when there is a genuine safety concern.

6. Therapists must create a neuroception of safety if emotional flooding occurs to help children get back into their windows of tolerance.

I am asking you to make the shift from seeing aggression as bad and needing to "do something to" the child to learning how to *be* with the child. I am asking you to move into the world of the right-brain experience, and in order to do this, you must learn how to *feel* what is happening between you and the child.

CHAPTER 2 KEY POINTS

- Aggression is a symptom of sympathetic nervous system activation when a child perceives a threat or challenge. It is a normal biological response.
- Understanding what aggression means takes the confusion out of what to do with aggression and makes the playroom a safe place to express the aggression.
- Integration, not catharsis, is the goal and objective of aggression in the playroom.
- Children are often given the message that aggression

is wrong and not acceptable, but what we suppress, we eventually express. In an attempt to stop the aggression, we may be promoting it.

- Shame and messages that aggression is not OK can result in children learning not to trust themselves and a disconnected relationship with the urges in their bodies.

- The core question that we need to be asking is "How do we teach children to recognize and manage the aggressive urges in their bodies without shaming them or promoting disconnection from their experience?"

Understanding the Nervous System

We use the relationship to allow our clients "to re-experience dysregulating affects in affectively tolerable doses in the context of a safe environment, so that overwhelming traumatic feelings can be regulated and integrated into the patient's emotional life."

Allan Schore (2003, p. 37)

UNDERSTANDING HOW THE BRAIN AND THE NER-vous system process information gives us more insight into what is going on when a child becomes aggressive or plays aggressively in a play therapy session. Knowing how the brain and the nervous system interpret information and influence symptoms in the body also helps us work with a child's behaviors and impulses that we might tradition-ally judge as "bad." It helps us understand that in addition to helping children integrate their traumatic memories and experiences, working with aggression also requires a repat-

terning of children's nervous systems and a deeper understanding of our role in the playroom.

Put your thinking caps on—it is time to jump into the
brain!

According to Joe Dispenza, author of *Evolve Your Brain:
The Science of Changing Your Mind* (2007), our brain processes 400,000,000,000 bits of sensory data per second. Our
brains are constantly taking in and processing sensory data
related to our external environment—what we see, smell,
feel, hear, and taste—as well as sensory data related to our
internal environment—our hormone levels, glucose levels,
heart rate, body temperature, etc.

This is an extraordinary amount of information for
our brains to integrate, and here's the really amazing part:
We're consciously aware of only 2,000 bits of it (Dispenza,
2007). Pause for a moment and consider the relevance of that
detail. If we're aware of less than 1% of all sensory data, the
majority of what we experience isn't even on our conscious
radar. We're not consciously aware of the vast majority of
information we take in. We register it on an implicit level,
which means that our body registers it, but we're not mentally aware of it. The reason this is so significant is that in
the playroom, therapists feel so much more than they allow
themselves to be consciously aware of. Whether your conscious mind registers it or not, your body is aware of what's
happening and is responding accordingly.

Once all this sensory data enters our brains, it makes its
way up to the amygdala, situated in the limbic area of the

brain. The amygdala plays a very important role—it's the part of the brain that determines whether the data it receives is identified as a possible threat. It makes an immediate decision about whether a threat is or isn't present based on past experience and knowledge. It's asking, "Have I seen this data before? Do I know anything about this data? Do I need to be scared? Do I need to protect myself? What do I know about this combination of sensory data?" If the amygdala decides there's a threat, it will send a signal to activate the autonomic nervous system, telling it to respond.

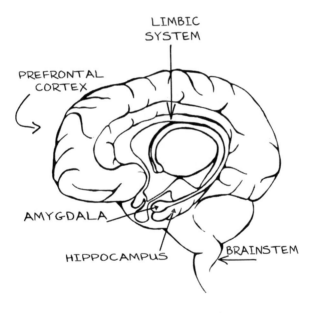

Have you ever wondered why people in the same situation can have different responses to a traumatic event? Or how one child can have more symptoms than his or her siblings even though they were all raised in the same environment? Or how one child can walk away from a tragic situation with little dysregulation and another walks away with post-traumatic stress disorder (PTSD) symptoms? Trauma is entirely dependent on the perception of the event and on whether we are able to integrate the data.

OUR NERVOUS SYSTEM'S DEFINITION OF A THREAT

When we hear the word *threat*, we tend to think of something that's challenging our physical safety, but the amygdala's definition of a threat is much broader than that. I have identified three other threats that the brain is attempting to find. In addition to scanning sensory data for what could be a physical threat, the brain is on alert for the unknown. This is the second threat the brain is scanning for, because the brain likes to know. It likes predictability. When it can't find predictability, it gets scared.

Reflection

Think of a time when you encountered the unknown. Maybe you were traveling and interacting with a culture that was completely foreign to you. Maybe you were eating at a restaurant, and when the waiter set your plate in front of you, you couldn't quite tell what was on it. Maybe you lost a job and woke up the next day not knowing what was going to happen next. If you mentally take yourself back to a moment when you've encountered the unknown, you'll recall that you paused for a second. That's a normal and necessary response.

When you think back about the particular "unknown" you recalled, you'll probably agree that it wasn't the unknown itself that was scary—it was the associations and memories about the possibilities of what could occur in the unknown that were scary. We project our past unintegrated experiences into the unknown, and this is where the sense of threat gets activated.

The third threat or challenge the brain is scanning for is incongruence in the environment. Let's go back to the story I shared in Chapter 1. When I was sword fighting with Carlos, I wasn't being congruent. I was role-playing, which is what I had been taught to do in my play therapy training. I wasn't giving myself permission to say out loud how I really felt when the sword was coming at me hard and fast. And I definitely wasn't regulating through it. I was just taking it, and as I was taking it, I was becoming less grounded. The result was that he kept amping it up. Why? Because I was incongruent. I was giving him mixed signals. My nonverbals were screaming that I was scared, but the rest of me was trying to stay cool and collected. I was part of the threat! He had to amp it up until he got an authentically congruent response from me.

Have you ever noticed what happens to your body and emotions when someone "shoulds" you or you "should" yourself? Stop and think about it for a moment. What happens when you hear messages like "You should spend more time doing this" or "You shouldn't act like that"? What happens when you tell yourself, "I shouldn't feel that way" or "I shouldn't have said that"?

Reflection

Think of a "should" that you've been saying to yourself recently. Close your eyes and say your "should" to yourself a few times, and observe what happens in your body. If you observe closely, you'll notice that you probably experienced some degree of dysregulation. Agitation, irritation, aggression, defensiveness, fatigue, depression, tightness and heaviness in the body, quickening of the heart rate, and hopelessness are all common experiences.

"Shoulds" and "unmet expectations" are the fourth threat or challenge because they're perceived as a danger to our sense of self. Nobody likes to be told that they should be different from who they are. When we "should" ourselves or we internalize the "shoulds" that we hear from others, we're directly challenging our authentic self. We're denying who we are in the moment and not seeing our own wisdom. This can create an internal dilemma between who we are and who we think we should be. The result is that the autonomic nervous system becomes activated trying to handle the discrepancy, and aggression can be one of the symptoms.

The number one thing that will block your ability to facilitate children through their aggression are the messages in your head about what you think you "should" or "shouldn't" do in the moment.

The four threats:

1. Physical pain,
2. The unknown,

3. Incongruence in the environment,

4. "Shoulds" and "unrealistic expectations."

THE NERVOUS SYSTEM IN ACTION

The autonomic nervous system has two sides: a sympathetic branch for revving us up and a parasympathetic branch for slowing us down. They work in tandem to support overall healthy functions of the body. When we perceive one of the four threats just explored, the autonomic nervous system will move into excessive responses of the sympathetic and dorsal parasympathetic branches to help us deal with the threat or challenge at hand. This is referred to as *nervous system dysregulation*. The sympathetic nervous system is responsible for our freeze, fight, and flight responses (hyper-aroused), while the dorsal parasympathetic branch is responsible for our collapse response, also referred to as the faint response (hypo-aroused).

Have you ever wondered why someone goes into a freeze, fight, or flight response instead of a collapse response, or vice versa? Did you know that there's a choice? It turns out that the branch we choose is based on our perception of these threats or challenges. If we perceive that we can do something about it, our sympathetic branch initiates our flight-or-fight system. Our energy will travel from the core of our body to our arms, legs, feet, and hands so we can run or fight. We can actually feel the energy in our hands and feet, and we start moving. We also get a surge of energy to our

SYNERGETIC
PLAY THERAPY™

Nervous System Symptoms of Regulation and Dys-regulation

All symptoms of dys-regulation arise out of mis-perceptions of the events in our lives. When we change our perceptions, we change the symptoms in our nervous system. It wise to master the art of how to change our perceptions and how to manage the symp toms that arise in our bodies to help return us to a more regulated/ventral state.

Sympathetic Response— Freeze, Flight, Fight Hyper-arousal Symptoms	Parasympathetic/Ventral Vagal Response–Regulated Symptoms (Mindful/ "Attached to Self")	Parasympathetic/Dorsal Vagal Response—Collaps Hypo-arousal Symptoms
Hyper-alert		Helplessness
Hyper-vigilant	Think logically/clearly	Appear life-less
Increased heart rate	Able to make conscious choices	Non-expressive
Defensive	Able to make eye contact	Numbing
"Pounding" sensation in the head	Display a wide range of emotional expression	Lack of motivation
Anxious	Feel "grounded"	Lethargic/Tired
Excessive Motoric Activity	Able to notice breath	Dulled capacity to feel significant events
Overwhelmed, Disorganized	Sleep Cycles Stable	Emotional constriction
Highly irritable	Poised	Depression
Uncontrollable bouts of rage	Internal awareness of both mind and body	Isolation
Aggressive	"In the body"	Dissociation
Dissociation	Able to communicate verbally in a clear manner	

©2011 Lisa Dion, LPC, RPT-S Updated 1/2018

ergetic Play Therapy™ — Regulation Activities

:d below are just some examples of activities that can be used to help regulate a
regulated nervous system. It is wise to do these activities pro-actively, as well as in
ients of dys-regulation. It is also important to follow the body's innate wisdom back to a
lated/ventral state. These activities are important to be done alone AND with someone.

jump, spin, e with pauses ke deep breaths.	Eat (particularly something crunchy)	Walk quickly	Swing
e a game and have jump high to h something high wall or in a door e	Drink through a straw	Run up and down steps	Learn about "Brain Gym"—tons of ideas
	Take a bath or shower	Shake head quickly	Yoga
	Wrap up in a blanket and snuggle (a little tightly for some pressure)—of course, do this safely.	Hang upside down off of a bed or couch	Snuggle
jump, etc and h into something (i.e jump on a bed crash repeatedly)		Play sports	Dance
	March or sing during transitions	"Doodle" on paper (this one can be a bit more distracting, but sometimes works)	Move, move, move— any way that it feels good to your body
nce on a yoga ball	Play Mozart music in the background during challenging times of the day if in hyper-arousal	Hold or fidget a Koosh ball, rubber band, straw, clay	Describe what is happening in your body out loud—"My tummy is going in circles", "My legs feel heavy", etc. . . .
across the floor and forth		Rub gently or vigorously on your skin or clothing	
a chair and push vith your arms (as ing to get out of chair)—keep some tance	Play Hard Rock/ Fast/Bass music if in hypo-arousal	Put a cold or hot wash cloth on face	Breathe, breathe, breathe—make sure that your inhalation is the same length as your exhalation
sages	Carry heavy things or push heavy things around	Dim the lights if in hyper-arousal	
p pressure on s and legs (you can ly apply pressure n arms and legs in g stroking motion)	Do isometrics (wall pushups or push hands together (looks like you are praying))	Turn on the lights if in hypo-arousal	
		Read a book	

face and head. This primal response makes our face flush, our jaws tense, and our pupils dilate to take in data. Our heart rate increases. We're hyper-alert and hyper-vigilant, and we become both defensive and aggressive. If we are not able to get away from the threat or challenge, feelings of anxiety and panic start to set in. That's the essence of being hyper-aroused.

But what happens when we perceive the threat as overwhelming and believe we can't do anything about it? When we don't feel big enough, fast enough, loud enough, smart enough, or strong enough to combat the threat, our nervous system begins to shut down, going into a collapsed state. This hypo-aroused response is a sign of activation of the dorsal parasympathetic branch. At an extreme level, we can even faint and dissociate. When the kids in our playroom are dorsal activated, immobilization starts to manifest. They can seem tired, with not much affect or expression. At extreme levels, they're almost ghostlike and robotic; the lack of energy in their extremities makes them numb. That's an attempt to stop the pain, but it leads to emotional constriction and feelings of isolation and depression. These children are shut down. They're in the room, but nobody's home. The same series of events happens for us when we are dorsal activated.

It can be useful to conceptualize the activation of the autonomic nervous system as occurring in stages based on the degree of challenge in our perception. We begin in a freeze response as we orient to the potential threat. The freeze response in the sympathetic nervous system is short-lived, as its primary goal is to help us turn toward the data, pause, and gather more information to make a decision about what to do next. The second and third stages continue with sympathetic activation, allowing us to move into a fight-or-flight response Initially we will attempt to flee, but if we can't, we will engage our fight response. If we are not able to flee or fight, we can move into dual autonomic activation, with both sympathetic and dorsal activation. This is a bit like having one foot on the accelerator and one foot on the brake. We can't figure out what to do, but we haven't quite collapsed yet. It is at this point that some dissociation can start to occur. If there is still no resolution to the threat or challenge, we will move into the next phase, which is the collapse response of the dorsal parasympathetic branch. As we perceive that we can't do anything about the situation, our system will start to shut down, and our movements will become slower, our heart rate and blood pressure will drop, and if it happens quickly, we can faint (Schwartz & Maiberger, 2018; Elbert & Schauer, 2010).

When I was in the sword fight with Carlos, my brain was taking in a lot of sensory data. That data made its way to my amygdala, at which point it quickly assessed whether there was a possible threat. The decision was a definite "Yes!" At that point, a signal was sent to activate my autonomic nervous system to do something about the perceived challenge.

At first, my brain perceived that I could do something about it, so I had a hyper-aroused response and attempted to fight back. Since I was not regulating, setting boundaries, or having an authentic response, and Carlos began to speed up and intensify the swings coming at me, I started to believe I couldn't do anything about it, and I began to check out in a hypo-aroused response. This all occurred within minutes, and then—*bam*—I got hit in the head. To this day, I still have no idea what he hit me with.

Therapists who perceive threats as they deal with the intense aggression in the playroom for an extended period of time without regulating and managing their own perceptions will probably begin to manifest signs of hypo-arousal in their own bodies that will carry over into their lives outside of the playroom. Our nervous systems can handle only so much. Over time they will show signs of dorsal parasympathetic activation as their system starts to shut down.

NEUROCEPTION OF SAFETY

There is another part of the parasympathetic branch that is significant to understand. This is the ventral branch of the vagus nerve. Stephen Porges's polyvagal theory brought to light that both the dorsal branch and the ventral branch of the vagus nerve serve to support the body to slow down; however, they do so for very different reasons. As I just described, our dorsal activation is in response to a perception of a threat. This is in contrast to ventral activation, which arises when we have a "neuroception" of safety (Porges, 2011; Badenoch, 2017). Think of the ventral vagal nerve like a brake system. In fact, it is sometimes referred to as the *ventral brake*. When engaged, it helps put the brake on the dysregulation and gives us access to a greater regulatory capacity. It also helps keep us in our window of tolerance, the optimal zone of arousal that allows a person to integrate sensory data (Ogden, Minton & Pain, 2006; Siegel, 1999), which is the optimal zone of arousal of our nervous system activation (Siegel, 2012). Learning ways to regulate, as demonstrated in this book, will help you keep your ventral branch engaged. This engagement will allow you to be in the experience with the child without getting emotionally flooded. It also helps children feel safe, as they can sense that you are grounded in the intensity and present and attuned with them.

NERVOUS SYSTEMS IN THERAPY

It's more common for children who are hyper-aroused to be referred to play therapy, but we need to make sure we aren't forgetting about the hypo-aroused children and educate parents and teachers about the need for these children to receive support. Sometimes these kids are overlooked because they're easy and compliant, but we need to keep in mind that they are in a hypo-aroused state, which means their perception is that the challenges are too big and they've already begun to shut down their emotional worlds. This is in contrast with the child who's acting out and therefore still believes he has a chance.

We all work with kids who have been diagnosed with

or show signs of having a wide range of disorders, including oppositional defiant disorder, conduct disorder, anxiety disorders, bipolar disorder, post-traumatic stress, attention deficit disorders, and depressive disorders. What's fascinating is to consider the idea that every symptom and diagnosis a child brings into therapy is the result of a dysregulated nervous system.

Maybe instead of diagnosing our kids with a disorder, the diagnosis needs to be, "He's dysregulated in excessive sympathetic activation" or "She's dysregulated in excessive dorsal parasympathetic activation." How would we approach our child clients in the playroom if we viewed them through this lens? How would this change the way we support parents and teachers when they're struggling with a child?

The child's symptoms are understood as symptoms of dysregulated states of the nervous system.
                                        —*Synergetic Play Therapy* tenet

Understanding the symptoms of the nervous system when a threat or challenge is perceived can give us insight into the child's perception of how big the challenge is. It also gives us information regarding our own perceptions when we begin to experience symptoms. It is important to note that when aggression shows up in the playroom, we are most likely interacting with the hyper-aroused sympathetic activation. However, this isn't always the case. Sometimes we will see dorsal activation in the playroom. Understanding the various symptoms of dysregulation of the nervous system and the sequence of stages of activation is critical. Knowing this helps us track escalation and overwhelm and monitor emotional flooding within ourselves and within the child.

NERVOUS SYSTEMS IN AGGRESSIVE PLAY

Very simply put, when aggressive play begins to show up in the playroom, you can know that the child's nervous system is simultaneously hyper-aroused. You might even think of the play itself as the symbolic representation of the sympathetic activation of the nervous system. This happens because as children begin to play, their associated memories and bodily sensations will arise. As a result, they'll begin to show signs of dysregulation in their nervous systems as they attempt to work with the challenging information that's coming up for them.

When the children or the play becomes aggressive and intense, it simply means that their nervous systems are moving into a highly activated sympathetic response. It's interesting to note that often, the sympathetic and dorsal parasympathetic energies show up in pairs in the playroom. As examples, just at the moment that the aggressive energy has reached its peak as the child corners the therapist and shoots him (hyper-aroused), the therapist begins to die, lose power, and become helpless (hypo-aroused). In observational play, the same is true. As the war in the sand tray reaches a high state of chaos and aggression (hyper-aroused), the soldiers under fire begin to die, and many even fall over or disappear under the sand (hypo-aroused).

When we understand that the play that emerges when aggression shows up is both the symbolic form and an extension of the extreme arousal states of a child's nervous system, we can embrace a paradigm for healing based on nervous system regulation: All behavior, including aggression, is an attempt at regulation. This isn't to say that a child's play is never literal and that when children are playing aggressively they aren't reenacting a past experience. What I am saying is that there is a lot more going on besides this reenactment, and once we can embrace a paradigm of viewing children's symptoms through the lens of neuroscience and nervous system states, new opportunities for healing and integration arise.

CHAPTER 3 KEY POINTS

- The amygdala is the filter of threat versus nonthreat in the brain—scanning for physical threats, the unknown, incongruences in the environment, and "should" messages. It is important to keep these threats in mind as we facilitate aggression in the playroom.
- Two branches of the autonomic nervous system are present in life and in the playroom: the sympathetic branch, which revs us up, and the parasympathetic branch, which slows us down.

- Aggressive play is both the symbolic form of and an extension of the extreme sympathetic activation in a child's nervous system.

- Your beliefs about what you "should" or "shouldn't" do when aggression arises in the playroom can block your ability to facilitate the moment.

- Your perception about whether or not you can do something about a threat or challenge activates you toward sympathetic arousal or dorsal collapse.

- When we help children move toward their intense emotional states and sensations, we're developing resiliency in the children while helping to repattern their nervous systems.

What Regulation Really Means

THE MORE THERAPISTS I TEACH, THE MORE AWARE I become that the concept of regulation or becoming regulated is often misunderstood. Many people think that being regulated means being calm, but that isn't always the case. From a Synergetic Play Therapy perspective, regulated means I'm mindful and aware of myself. In a moment of regulation, I can think clearly, I can make a conscious choice, I'm able to notice my breath, I'm able to feel grounded, I can speak clearly, and I have an experience of being *in my body*. I'm connected to myself. (Refer to the nervous system chart in Chapter 3.)

Regulation in the nervous system occurs when we become consciously aware of ourselves and our ventral vagal nerve is activated. In those moments, we're aware that we're separate from whatever is happening. We know that we're not the anger or the sadness. We're larger than that experience, if only for a brief moment. That moment of awareness empowers us to attach to ourselves and connect to others. We can therefore be regulated in our anger. We can be regulated in our sadness. We can be regulated in our anxiety. We can also be regulated when others are having challenging emotions around us.

As an example, let's say something totally irritates me. My perception of the challenge causes me to become dysregulated and detach from myself. I end up in a state of hyperarousal, and I'm not at all connected to myself. I'm feeling consumed by the sensation of irritation inside me. Then I become aware. I notice that I'm talking faster. I notice I'm tapping my fingers, my right leg is moving, and my heart rate is picking up. I notice that my body feels activated inside. As the activation intensifies, I get a little dizzy. I start to notice and pay attention to everything I feel and see. As I do, I begin to come back to myself. I'm no longer detached. I can feel the intensity coursing through my body, and I'm aware. I'm having moments of regulation during the intensity, and I definitely don't feel calm. This is the type of regulation we're trying to teach our child clients. We want them to learn how to reattach to themselves when they become dysregulated so that they can manage the intensity that occurs inside them.

REGULATION EXISTS ON A CONTINUUM

You may have a brief moment of regulation or you may have many moments of regulation that add up to a state of regulation, in which you may feel calm. In the example I just gave, I was having moments of regulation. I mention this because it's important that as play therapists we understand that becoming calm is neither the goal nor the point of learning how to facilitate aggressive play in the playroom. The point is to learn how to manage the energy of our dysregulated states and to teach children how to do the same. Understanding this is key to doing this work. If your goal is to stop the energy because you want the energy to calm down, you will inadvertently shut the child's process down or contain the child in a way that may encourage the energy to remain stuck or spinning within the child rather than being integrated. Remember that whatever we repress must get expressed somewhere.

Rather than stopping the energy in the playroom, let's teach our clients how to regulate through the intensity by teaching them to become mindful of their experience. This allows them to move toward their experience instead of running away from it, which can escalate the symptoms. It's through self-awareness that the energy in the aggressive play will begin to integrate, and over time the child will naturally arrive at a state of regulation.

We regulate to move toward the intensity, not to get out of it.

It's not practical to think that children will never rage again, never want to hit their friend again, or never talk back to an adult again. There will probably also be times when children want to run and hide and put their heads under the covers and never come out again. What is practical and possible is teaching kids how to stay connected to themselves when they're faced with challenges. This is what facilitating aggressive play is all about. We want to help children stay connected to themselves (ventral engagement) during the intensity of their hyper- and hypo-aroused states so that they can integrate the energy and become self-aware. We want to teach them that they can feel it and notice it without being consumed by it.

CHILDREN ARE NATURAL REGULATORS

All behavior is an attempt at regulation, even the behaviors that society might label "inappropriate." Children bite, hit, yell, push, throw tantrums, hide, avoid making eye contact, and refuse to talk in an attempt to regulate by bringing in or shutting out sensory data. Children also wiggle, sing, roll around on the floor, jump, push against things, hang upside down, play, create art, and engage in many other actions to regulate. They're brilliant and will do whatever is necessary to manage the emotions and sensations that are arising in their bodies. This includes becoming aggressive. It may be a paradigm shift to consider aggressive behavior as an attempt at regulation.

The challenge occurs when children's strategies for regulation aren't effective, keeping them in a state of dysregulation, and when their regulation strategies are negatively affecting their lives. The more time a child spends in the freeze/flight/fight/collapse response, the higher the probability that the child will experience problems in areas such as health, relationship, learning, rage and depression, and impulsivity.

Although children have a natural instinct to regulate, they need help with learning how to regulate effectively. In other words, they need help learning how to engage their ventral state to manage their dysregulation. One of the primary ways they seek out help is by watching how others manage their emotions and bodily sensations.

In the playroom, this translates into needing the therapist to show them what to do with the aggressive urges in their bodies.

THE NEED FOR AN EXTERNAL REGULATOR

I am going to ask a question. The answer will help you understand why I have chosen to explore the role of the therapist as the most important element in making aggressive play therapeutic.

Why do we rock babies when they are in distress?

The answer may seem so intuitively obvious that you want to just keep reading, but take a moment and really think about this. Do we rock babies to physically soothe the pain in their bodies? To help settle the emotional distress they are feeling inside? To help them know they are not alone? To help them know they can trust that their needs will get met, at least most of the time? To help them know that it is OK to ask for their needs to be met? Of course the answer is yes!

What about helping the babies begin to learn about the sensations in their bodies? Helping the babies learn how to connect to themselves in the midst of challenging emotional states? What about to lay down the wiring in the brain as the babies learn what it feels like to move from a dysregulated state to a regulated state over and over again, creating a template for a strong regulatory capacity? The answer to these questions is also yes.

When a baby is highly dysregulated, an attuned caregiver doesn't ask the baby to take a deep breath or to focus on something that feels calming or to count to ten. This seems so obvious, as we know that a baby can't do this. We understand that babies are responding from more primitive parts of their brains and haven't yet built a strong ability to self-soothe. We understand that babies need the help of an external regulator, someone who can help them organize their internal experiences. We understand that an attuned caregiver must lead.

When babies are born, their capacity to self-soothe is still immature in its development. Babies need the support of an attuned caregiver to learn how to return to a state of regulation. We might even say that babies borrow the regulatory capacity of the caregiver as their own regulatory capacity develops. Allan Schore stated that "the mother is literally a regulator of the crescendos and de-crescendos of the baby's developing autonomic nervous system" (Bullard, 2015). We forget that many of the children we work with are babies disguised in big bodies, and we expect them to be able to regulate in ways that they can't in the moment or maybe never learned how to do. We also forget that when children are playing through traumatic experiences and the corresponding activation arises in their nervous systems, they, too, need support to regulate through the intensity. To sum this up, in order to help repattern children's nervous systems, the children first need an external regulator, someone to help integrate the dysregulated state in their nervous systems. Integrating intensity must first start with the therapist.

When Adrianne and I began working together, she was 12 years old, chronologically. She was brought to me as a last-ditch effort, as she had been in and out of various therapies, including play therapy, since she was 5, with very few results.

Adrianne was adopted at 4 years old from Russia. When she came to see me, she came with a combined diagnosis of autism, reactive attachment disorder, attention deficit disorder, and various developmental delays. Her parents also suspected abuse in her early years before they adopted her. She was incredibly reactive emotionally, often hitting her parents, hitting herself, and hurting the pets in the home. She had difficulty resting and sleeping, as her nervous system seemed to live in an ongoing fight-or-flight response. As expected, she also had a difficult time trusting, making eye contact, and staying with an activity for an extended period of time. She was constantly moving. Her parents described being with her like hanging out with a time bomb that could go off at any moment. After years of living with her aggression, they no longer felt safe around her.

During our first few sessions, Adrianne's play was filled with aggression, overwhelm, and fear, as babies and animals were repeatedly hurt and even terrorized. As she played, I observed her nervous system go in and out of sympathetic activation. I felt the activation in my own body as well as I observed and tracked her play. I also saw how hard it was for her to connect to herself and settle. The unintegrated trauma she was holding in her system created the fear that it wasn't safe to fully let go. It also kept her in a fight-or-flight state.

When I met with her parents, I shared with them that in order for us to help her, we were going to have to help repattern her nervous system, in addition to helping her integrate the experiences she'd had in her life that registered for her as traumatic. I explained the brain and the nervous system states to them and helped them understand that she was responding from the primitive parts of her brain, and her capacity to regulate her internal experience was not high, which was contributing to her inability to settle and to her aggressive behavior. I also shared that although she was chronologically 12, she was actually at the emotional age of an infant. I shared my hope and belief that I could help.

Adrianne needed the help of an external regulator in the playroom in order to help her integrate the intensity she was experiencing inside and to help rewire her brain toward a greater regulatory capacity. I needed to become this for her, and I also was going to have to teach her parents how to do the same.

Each time the intensity and aggression arose in Adrianne's play, I practiced what I am going to teach you to do in this book. I engaged in various regulatory activities to help me move toward the intensity in the playroom and to begin to work with her regulatory system. I also made a lot of observational statements regarding what she was doing and what she was playing with in order to help her orient.

When she placed the baby alone in the dollhouse, I said, "The baby is all alone." The baby then started to crawl toward the banister on the second floor and climb it. "There is no one in the house to protect the baby from falling off the banister." She then grabbed the baby and threw it off the second floor. "The baby fell!" The baby then lay there, not moving. "The baby might be hurt! No one is there to help the baby. The baby is all alone and possibly hurting." These were the types of observational statements I made to help track her play and let her know that I was with her and following her play. She was nonverbal the entire session, and as she played, I continued to track her.

As a baby or animal would get hurt in the play, she would quickly switch and create another play scene where another baby or animal would get hurt. This was a continuous process that involved no pause, which meant there wasn't time for her nervous system to rest. Her nervous system stayed sympathetically activated.

I also noticed as she played that my body wanted to rest in the midst of all of the sympathetic activation, but it couldn't, as the play went from one traumatic scene to another. I soon realized that this was her world. It wasn't that she didn't want to rest; she literally couldn't. It wasn't safe to, because in her mind, something bad might happen. In the context of the play, I described the experience of my body to her. "I am noticing that my body wants to rest. It wants to pause, but it can't. My body feels like it needs to stay alert." And then I would take a huge breath and elongate my exhalation. The elongation of my breath was a message to Adrianne that it was OK to begin to let go and allow her own nervous system to settle. It was also a way to support the regulation of my own nervous system and keep me in a ventral state of activation. The most important part about this story is that it was during the moments when I became incredibly present and regulated and was authentic about my experience that Adrianne would look at me and attempt to make eye contact. She was tuning in, borrowing the regulation in my nervous system, and it helped her feel safe. This was the turning point in our work together, as I started to see the beginning signs of her nervous system starting to settle.

The therapist's ability to become the external regulator also helps the child's play integrate rather than stay repetitive. It was the addition of my own regulation in her play and my willingness to share my experience with Adrianne that allowed her to feel felt by me. My attunement, first to myself and then to her, allowed her to attune to me, borrow the regulation of my nervous system, and then attune to herself. This was when the play shifted and the repetition stopped.

On session four, Adrianne came in and announced in the play that it was time for the baby to sleep. The baby slept for 15 seconds. It was a start. Over the next few sessions, we worked on resting. Adrianne became the baby in the play. As she would lie down to sleep, she would become anxious. As her external regulator, I continued to breathe. Sometimes I would hum a song. Sometimes I would gently rock, sitting next to her. Knowing that she was tuning in to me, I stayed deeply connected and in tune with her while staying connected to myself, and each time she borrowed my regulatory capacity. I couldn't pick her up and rock her as an infant (although had she wanted this, I would have found a way to create this experience for her with a lot of safety, since I didn't know exactly what type of abuse she might have experienced early on), but I could still do all of things that an attuned caregiver would have done with her to help her rest and feel safe. I remember the day that I walked out of the play therapy room to the waiting room to find her mom. When I saw her, I looked at her and said, "She fell asleep." Her mom had tears in her eyes, as she understood the significance of this. Her mom came back to the room and sat and breathed with Adrianne for the next 15 minutes while she slept until it was time to go.

You might be wondering what this has to do with integrating aggression. The answer is everything.

CHAPTER 4 KEY POINTS

- Regulation occurs in a moment of mindful awareness. It does not necessarily mean being calm.
- All behavior is an attempt at regulation, including
  aggression.
- During a play therapy session, children borrow the
  regulatory capacity of the therapist as they attempt to
  integrate their challenging internal states.
- Integrating intensity starts with the therapist becoming the external regulator.
- Becoming calm is not the goal of facilitating aggression in the playroom; the goal is helping children stay
  connected to themselves in the midst of their dysregulation so they can learn to feel it without becoming
  consumed by it.

Developing Yourself as the External Regulator

As you are probably starting to discover, this book is really about your ability to hold the intensity in the room as it arises, allowing children to move toward their internal states. This and your ability to become the external regulator are what support the child's capacity to integrate the intensity, making aggressive play therapeutic. I said in Chapter 1 that this work starts with you. It begins with you moving out of a paradigm that teaches you to be a neutral observer, into a role where you become an active participant in the therapeutic dyad.

What I am proposing and outlining is not easy work, but it is necessary work. In this chapter, I am going to walk you through various steps you can take to begin to help yourself widen your window of tolerance around aggression and begin to develop your capacity to be an external regulator.

COMMITMENT TO GROWTH

Being a play therapist is not just a commitment to the children we work with but also a commitment to ourselves and our ongoing personal growth. If we are going to take on the courageous role of helping children heal, we must be actively engaged in healing ourselves. Choosing to work with children requires us to continue to strengthen our capacity to hold what the child is bringing to the session. We need to learn how to stay connected to ourselves and our clients in the midst of the uncomfortable thoughts, feelings, and sensations that arise in the session without avoiding or merging with our clients. It is normal during a child's play that we will naturally want to move toward some of the play and away from other play depending on the level of threat that our brains perceive. For this reason, a continual look at our own relationships and histories with aggression, and what still needs healing within us, is necessary.

Developing the capacity to become the external regulator during aggressive play requires two main things:

1. Therapists must be willing to *feel* what is happening in their own bodies without wanting to avoid or become consumed by the experience.
2. Therapists must work through their own fears and past experiences related to aggression.

FEEL IT TO ATTUNE

Becoming an external regulator requires the ability to attune. To attune to our clients, we must be open to our own bodily and emotional states (Schore, 1994; Siegel, 2007). This means we need to stop trying to figure everything out in the playroom and begin to feel what's happening. I tell my students to get out of their heads and get into their bodies. Through your body, you will be able to access all the information necessary to facilitate what's needed in that moment. Think of it this way: When a baby is screaming, attuned caregivers don't stop and analyze the situation and try to figure out the best intervention for soothing the baby—they instinctually pick up the baby and begin to rock, sway, make sounds, bounce, and follow their instincts about what to do next. There's no map, just moment-to-moment attunement that reveals what to do. For caregivers to do this effectively, they're feeling their way through each moment. Facilitating aggressive play is very similar.

Feel your way through the play—don't think your way through the play.

Josh, age 5, put a baby in my arms, handed me a doctor kit, and then walked over to the window in my office, leaving me on the other side of the room. My initial response was confusion. Why had I just been handed a baby? What was I supposed to do with this doctor kit? Why had he walked away and was now staring out the window? In the midst of all of my internal questioning, he looked at me and said, "Come on, Lisa . . . You are supposed to be anxious!" I had been so caught up in the confusion of the moment and trying to figure it out that I didn't let myself drop into feeling what I was experiencing. I wasn't attuned to myself or to him because I was so busy trying to analyze what was going on. I was disconnected from my body in that moment. This kept me from feeling what he was trying to set me up to feel. Josh had to stop his play to help me get it. This example highlights what happens when the therapist is not willing to *feel*. Not only does the child feel "missed," but the child also has to spend more time helping the therapist "get it."

This moment of misattunement also wasn't a bad thing, as it offered him a chance to advocate for his needs to be met, which is a hugely beneficial skill for him to have in relationship.

As soon as I heard his words, I put my attention into my body and became present with him and in the play. The moment I did, I felt the anxiety he was trying to get me to register. He wanted me to feel anxious not knowing if the baby was OK or not. Josh helped me get it so that I could get him. He wanted me to feel what it felt like to be him, and he did this by orienting me toward my experience so that he could get an authentic emotional response from me.

Attuning to Josh began with attuning to myself.

MOVE TOWARDS THE INTENSITY

When a client's painful memories and emotional states are reactivated and are outside the client's window of tolerance, the client will begin to move away from those emotions in an attempt to avoid the intensity (Siegel, 2010). The act of moving away from the experience reinforces the message in the brain that there is a threat or a challenge, which keeps the nervous system in a state of dysregulation. The same is true for us. If we aren't willing to experience our own bodily, emotional, and cognitive states while working toward modulating these inner experiences, we'll move away from these states (Schore, 1994), potentially leaving our client feeling unsafe and unseen (Siegel, 2010).

When therapists are not able or willing to feel the shifts that are occurring inside of themselves during the play, they will have a high probability of moving away from those particular emotions or body sensations, shutting them down in some way, denying their existence, or emotionally flooding. Moving toward the intensity requires therapists to feel what is happening in their bodies while simultaneously regulating through it. Dales & Jerry (2008) describe the importance of the therapist moving toward difficult and intense states like this.

Much like the mother who is implicitly modeling for the child her own struggles to regulate her own dysregulated state, the therapist must be able to resonate empathically with the clients, psychobiologically feeling their difficult, intense states. Without this ability to self-manage, the therapist cannot help the client to regulate. Such work implies a profound commitment by both participants in the therapeutic scenario and a deep emotional involvement on the therapist's part. (Dales & Jerry, p. 300)

Allan Schore also explained that the therapist's ability to regulate the child's arousal states requires the therapist to be able to pick up and attune to both the children's distress and negative emotional states, as well as their positive emotional states (Bullard, 2015). This means that for attunement to occur, therapists must be willing to move toward their internal experiences and be capable of feeling in their bodies the full range of what the child is feeling.

OUR VENTRAL EMBRACE

Let's be honest—feeling what is happening in our bodies during a play therapy session can be uncomfortable! And although it is uncomfortable, it is incredibly necessary.

In these moments, if we can't hold our own discomfort, we will have a hard time holding the child's. This is why it is so important to continue to develop a relationship with our bodies and to continue to widen our capacity to feel while staying connected to ourselves.

I want to highlight the importance of this by saying it another way. As children play and their uncomfortable thoughts, feelings, and sensations arise, they need our window of tolerance to be larger than theirs. In a sense, they need to be embraced by our regulatory capacity (Badenoch, 2017; Kestly, 2016). This allows them to go deeper into their feelings, knowing they are held by our ventral embrace. The following diagram found in Bonnie Badenoch's book *The Heart of Trauma* (2017) demonstrates the ventral embrace. The child's window of tolerance meets the therapist's window of tolerance to create a joined window of tolerance. At this point, the child can explore sympathetic arousal and dorsal collapse while being regulated by the therapist.

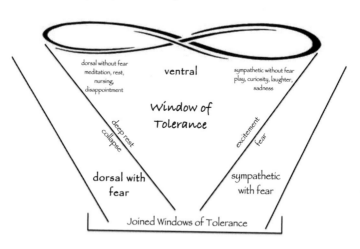

Autonomic Nervous System

Expanding and Contracting Joined Windows of Tolerance

"*Figure 5.2*" from THE HEART OF TRAUMA: HEALING THE EMBODIED BRAIN IN THE CONTEXT OF RELATIONSHIPS by Bonnie Badenoch. Copyright © 2018 by Bonnie Badenoch. Used by permission of W. W. Norton & Company, Inc.

As the children are held by our ventral embrace, the children will experience a widening of their windows of tolerance as we are able to hold the intensity. The research of Carl Marci and colleagues (2005) found these moments to be subjectively experienced as empathetically rich interpersonal joining. With this interpersonal joining our nervous systems will flow into, out of, and back into synchrony many times (Badenoch, 2011).

DEVELOP A RELATIONSHIP WITH YOUR BODY

In order to develop your capacity to feel and attune, it is important to spend time in your body (Van der Kolk, 2015). It is important to get to know the sensations and feelings that arise in you throughout the day. Your body is your most important tool as a therapist. It contains all of the information you need to understand what is happening in you, in your client, and between both of you in any given moment. Without a relationship with our bodies, we are fish out of water in the playroom.

It is also important to learn how to trust and listen to your body. For many people, this isn't so easy. There are many life experiences and messages that can contribute to a disconnected relationship with the body and a fear of spending time in the body. Abuse, medical trauma, messages about body image, and messages like "Get over it" when we are feeling angry or sad are examples of experiences that can contribute to the development of coping strategies to not feel.

If you have developed a disconnected relationship with your body, I invite you back home. If you have a strong relationship with your body, I invite you to continue to strengthen it.

There are many exercises you can do to strengthen your connection to your body and increase your ability to be with challenging emotional states. Here are a few of my favorites:

- **Yoga, martial arts, and mindful dancing:** As you move, allow yourself to become aware of the various sensations throughout your body. Take time to notice how your feet feel. How your hips feel. How your neck feels. As you notice parts of your body that are contracted or carry tension, take a breath and practice bringing your awareness deeper into those areas of your body. Also notice if there are parts of your body that you want to avoid paying attention to. Get curious about why.

- **Touch:** Receive touch from loved ones or through massage with a safe adult. As your body is being touched, allow yourself to notice your body. Notice the pressure or lack thereof when contact is made with your skin. Notice your muscles and your joints. Notice the thoughts that simultaneously arise as you are being touched. Note: If something about the touch is uncomfortable or your body would like a different experience, practice speaking up and naming your experience. It is your body, and you get to say no if you need to. You also get to ask for more of what you want and need.

- **Heighten your senses:** This can be done by engaging in various activities that stimulate your senses and mindfully paying attention to your experience. Examples include playing music and listening to the subtle changes in the rhythm while noticing the sounds from the various instruments. Choosing a food to mindfully eat is another exercise. As you eat it, slow down and focus on the texture, taste, and experience of the food in your mouth. Taking baths or swimming is another great activity, as it allows you to feel your body surrounded by the water and moving in the water. There are many examples; get creative.

- **Mindful breathing:** Sit alone for 10 minutes—sit with all of yourself. Take time to just sit, breathe, and notice. Notice the thoughts that arise as you sit and just witness. Notice the urge to get swept up in the stories you tell yourself. Notice the impulse to avoid or move toward different sensations in your body. Notice the emotions arising as you sit and see if you can just be with them, without changing them in any way.

- **Mindful walking:** One of my favorite practices is mindful walking in nature. As you walk outside, allow your attention to first enter your body. Begin to notice your breath and the quality of your breathing as you walk. Allow your mind to register what it feels like to walk as you begin to notice the sensa-

tion of each foot landing on the ground. Notice the
various sensations around your joints as they move.
Spend time in your body, just noticing. From there,
move your attention outside of yourself to bring in
the world around you. Feel the temperature on your
skin. Notice the colors that surround you. Let yourself tune in to the various shapes and movements of
whatever is in your view. Open your ears and listen.
Feel what it feels like to listen mindfully.

· **Pause, breathe, and feel:** As challenging emotions
arise, it is easy to simply react. I invite you to allow
yourself to pause as you begin to feel dysregulation in
your body. In this pause, breathe. Allow your attention to enter your body and feel the dysregulation.
Feel the energy inside of you. Take another breath and
lean in toward the discomfort. Breathe again and lean
in again. Just keep noticing as you breathe and feel.
At the moment you want to take your attention away,
challenge yourself to take one more breath and lean in
one more time. Feel a little deeper than last time.

These types of practices not only allow us to develop
a deeper relationship with ourselves, but they also help us
practice dual attention. Dual attention is the ability to be
aware of two things simultaneously. Developing dual attention is a necessary skill in therapy for attunement, as we need
to be aware of both ourselves and our clients in any given
moment. We also need to maintain awareness that although

we are having feelings and somatic shifts in response to the child's play, the story in the play isn't actually happening to us. If we are overly focused on our clients and their stories, we will lose connection with ourselves. If we are overly focused on ourselves and consumed by the emotions inside of us, we will lose connection with our clients.

You can practice dual attention in any of the activities that I have mentioned above by allowing yourself to become aware of yourself and something else outside of you at the same time. For example, while doing yoga, can you notice the sensations in your body during a pose while simultaneously noticing the other people around you (if you are in a yoga class)? You can practice dual attention in any activity that supports you in developing a deeper relationship with yourself and the world around you.

The key to beginning to expand your awareness and regulatory capacity is applying mindfulness to whatever you are doing and feeling. It is the act of becoming aware that teaches you how to "be with."

THE NEED TO RESCUE

There is a difference between being with children while they are in their discomfort, feeling the discomfort, and regulating alongside them, versus wanting to rescue the children out of their discomfort because we either believe that it isn't OK for them to be uncomfortable or we are too uncomfortable.

The first is integrative. The second is avoidance.

The need to rescue surfaces when we recognize in someone else, consciously or unconsciously, a part of ourselves that still needs healing. In these moments, it is common to try and redirect the play or children's experiences by avoiding being authentic if we fear that our authenticity would be too much for the children, asking the children questions that put them in their heads to avoid them feeling what is in their bodies, and directing the children away from certain play. These are strategies that are both an attempt to keep the children from feeling uncomfortable and also an attempt to help us feel comfortable, too.

When we look closely, we will often find that the inability to be with our uncomfortable thoughts, feelings, and sensations is rooted in fears that we have about what will happen if we were to feel them. An example of a fear might be, "If I allow myself to feel the intensity in my body, I will be consumed by it and I will start to cry in front of the child" or "If I feel the aggression in my own body, the child will see it and she won't like me or she will become scared of me." Often these fears are associated with experiences in our past that still need attention.

FACE YOUR FEARS

As we become afraid, our own protective patterns emerge, moving us out of connection with the child and into needing to protect ourselves from the child. Without mindful awareness and our own ability to regulate in these moments, our window of tolerance will shrink, leaving little capacity to support the child's regulation.

Learning how to face your fears builds your regulatory capacity, as it allows you to be able to maintain a neuroception of safety when the intensity arises. Simply put, the less scared you are, the more you can hold. This doesn't mean that you won't feel any fear in your body when aggression enters the playroom. It means that you can notice the fear in your body and stay ventrally activated, while at the same time thinking clearly about what you need to do and say without reacting. Facing your fears helps you respond instead of react. It also helps keep you present and connected.

How to Face Your Fears

A fear is the assumption that at some point in the future, you are going to experience more pain than pleasure, more bad than good, or more challenge than support. It is often connected to past experiences that, in our perception, did not go well, and of which we project the same or a similar outcome into the future (Demartini, 2010).

Reflection

Take out a piece of paper and write down all of the fears you have about children becoming aggressive in the playroom or their play becoming aggressive.

I am going to walk you through a simple but profound way to begin to integrate these fears so that you can stay more regulated and present in the playroom. I first learned this exercise in 2009 from Dr. John Demartini, my mentor, and it has been instrumental in helping shift and widen my window of tolerance. (Visit drdemartini.com for more information about Dr. Demartini or his work.)

This adapted exercise can be found in his book *Inspired Destiny* (2010, p. 139).

1. Consider what you're afraid of happening. For example, you might write, "I am afraid I will get emotionally flooded and set a boundary that sounds shaming."

2. Now come up with 20 to 50 benefits that you'd experience if this were to happen. For example, "I can repair with the child and model taking responsibility. It is an opportunity for me to learn about my window of tolerance and where I need to regulate more." Questions you can ask to help you discover the benefits are: "How does this fear coming true serve me, teach me, help me, and support my growth?" and "How does this fear coming true help my clients, teach my clients, and support their growth?"

3. Write down 20 to 50 drawbacks if the thing you fear doesn't happen. For example, "I wouldn't have the chance to repair with my client, which may have been a missed therapeutic moment that gives the child the opportunity to witness an adult take responsibility.

I wouldn't be forced to learn how to regulate, allowing me to be the child's external regulator during the intensity."

Once the brain can see that the worst-case scenario actually has benefits to you, the fear begins to integrate, allowing you to return to a more regulated state. This exercise is incredibly powerful, but it doesn't take away from the work you still need to do to integrate the past experiences that are contributing to the fear.

BELIEFS ABOUT AGGRESSION

Do you know what was discovered through the Adult Attachment Interview (AAI; PESI, 2012) as the best predictor of a child's level of attachment security with their caregiver? The answer may surprise you. The biggest predictor was how the adults were able to make sense of their own lives. It turns out that it wasn't what had happened to the adults but how the adults gave meaning to what they had been through that allowed them to tell a coherent and cohesive story of their pasts and how these experiences helped shape them into who they became. The adults who were securely attached themselves shared both positive and negative aspects of the events in their lives and how these influenced their developments and life journeys (Siegel, 1999).

The findings in the AAI revealed that the most important factor in attachment was the adults' abilities to understand how the events in their lives shaped them. The securely attached adults were able to make meaning of the challenging events in their lives.

A child is highly attracted to a therapist who displays this level of secure attachment with themselves in the playroom, because it means that they have a decreased need to rescue, avoid, or shut down the child's play. Instead, they can be present and grounded in the midst of the child's aggression, creating a sense of safety for the child as aggression arises.

This has significant relevance for play therapists working with aggression, because it means that our capacity to hold the intensity that arises when aggression enters the playroom is directly correlated to how well we have integrated the experiences in our own histories that feel similar. Another way of saying this is the more we have integrated from our past, the more we can hold in our present.

OUR PAST IN THE PLAYROOM

The bottom line is that our perceptions of our own aggression, witnessing aggression, and having aggression directed at us will influence our ability to stay present and grounded and to become the external regulator for the child.

If you have experiences in your history that are influencing your ability to stay present when aggression arises in the playroom, or you believe that aggression is a harmful, useless, purposeless experience that needs to be contained, shut down, or avoided, your need for it to stop will override the ability to implement any of the strategies and skills needed to transform it into a therapeutic experience.

Here are some questions to consider as you explore your beliefs about and relationship with aggression. My suggestion is that you spend time journaling, drawing, thinking about, and talking through the questions below to help you sort through your experiences.

- What is my current level of comfort with aggression in the playroom?
- Is it harder for me to witness aggressive play or to be an activate participant in aggressive play? Why?
- When aggression shows up in the playroom, what do I typically do? Why?
- What happens in my body when the child becomes aggressive in the playroom?
- When I think about aggression that I have experienced in my own life, what memories come to mind for me that still feel unresolved? What is the worst part of the memories?
- As a child, when I did something that was considered aggressive, what messages did I receive? How have these messages affected me and influenced my beliefs about aggression?
- Where in the past have I been the aggressor in my life? Am I carrying guilt or shame about this?
- Where in my current life do I display aggression? Am I carrying guilt or shame about this?

It is not what happens to us but how we make sense of what happens to us that ultimately matters most. How you think about your experiences with aggression influences your beliefs about aggression. If you believe that aggression is bad or scary, it will influence how you handle aggression when it shows up in the playroom. You will naturally carry more fears, and your protective patterns will have a higher probability of taking over. Your brain wants to keep you safe. If you are afraid of aggression, it is that much more important to practice what I am teaching you in this book so that you can work toward staying regulated when the fears arise and you start to feel dysregulated in session.

I encourage you to continue to do whatever healing work you need to do around your experiences with aggression. This is one of the greatest gifts you can give your child clients so that you can hold their aggression when it comes into the playroom. Your child clients are asking you to be present with them in their aggression, feeling what is happening in your own body and regulating through it so that you can become their external regulator, allowing them to borrow your regulatory capacity and work through their own aggression.

CHAPTER 5 KEY POINTS

- It is essential to develop a relationship with your body, as your body is your most important tool in the playroom.

- Attune: Feel your way through the play—don't think your way through the play.
- Your widow of tolerance needs to be larger than the children's in order to hold and help regulate their dysregulation.
- The urge to rescue or shut down the child's play is often correlated with the parts of ourselves that still need healing. Their pain reminds us of our pain.
- Your beliefs about whether or not aggression is bad, should be stopped, needs to be contained, and is scary will influence your ability to stay present when aggression shows up in the playroom.

6

The Basics of Regulating

IMAGINE THAT YOU'RE ABOUT TO GO SWIMMING AND the water is a bit cold. I go to the shores of Connecticut every summer, and even as I write this, I can feel the hairs on my arms stand up as I imagine the sensation of the cold water!

Now, I realize that you might be inclined to jump or dive into the water, but for this analogy, imagine that today you're feeling timid and your brain perceives the cold water as a challenge. You take a few steps into the water and immediately feel the cold water on your feet and ankles, and it's a little shocking! So you stop and breathe through the sensations, and as your body adjusts, you take another step out, and the water is now up to your knees. If you're anything like me, your shoulders are up to your ears and you're opening and closing your hands attempting to manage the sensations and probably saying, "Cold, cold, cold," or something less G-rated. After a few minutes, you adjust and take another step. The water is now up to your belly. This one is hard. The sensation is a little more intense, and you're tightening every muscle in your body, trying to handle the impact of the sensations. Again you breathe and try to help your body relax and adjust. Eventually, the temperature becomes tolerable and even refreshing. So it goes until eventually you're actually swimming.

Now let's look at what you automatically did to regulate as you moved into the cold water. First, you used mindfulness and awareness to develop a relationship with the sensations in your body. You also used breathing and movement to adjust to the intensity. You might even have yelled, shrieked, or named your experience out loud: "Ah! This is freezing!" These are all strategies you automatically used to regulate through the intensity and move farther out into the water until you were completely in it.

These are the exact same processes that can be used in the playroom. From a Synergetic Play Therapy perspective, therapists must first regulate their own bodies to keep themselves from experiencing high states of dysregulation, which can lead to burnout and symptoms of compassion fatigue. As we learned in the last chapter, it can also lead to an inability to stay present and wanting to shut the play down, which can lead to the child not feeling safe in the relationship. It also allows therapists to step into the role of the external regulator, allowing the child to borrow their regulatory capacity.

PUT YOUR OXYGEN MASK ON FIRST!

When we fly on an airplane, before we take off, the flight attendant gets on the speaker and announces the safety procedures to be followed in case of an emergency. One of the procedures we will hear is, "In case of loss of oxygen, an oxygen mask will fall from the compartment above you. If you're flying with a child or someone who needs help, please put your mask on before you assist them with theirs." Even airlines understand this principle. You have to help yourself breathe before you can help someone else! This principle is one of the foundations of learning how to teach regulation to your child clients.

You have to regulate yourself before you can help a child regulate.

As children play and their nervous systems become activated, their memories, emotions, and body sensations will begin to emerge. We'll feel the dysregulated states of their nervous systems through a process called *resonance*, whether we're consciously aware of it or not. Remember, our brains take in a lot more information than we consciously register. Resonance, as defined by Siegel (2012, p. AI-69), is "the mutual influence of interacting systems on each other that allows two or more entities to become a part of one functional whole."

The children need us to mindfully feel, so we can continue to attune and be present with them. The experience of being present can be described this way.

Presence involves being aware of what is happening as it is happening, being receptive to our own inner mental sea, and attuning to the inner life of another person. Being present for others means we resonate with what is going on in their inner worlds, creating the essential way we feel their feelings. (Siegel, 2013, p. 218)

In a session, when children are dysregulated, all of their nonverbal and verbal cues are offering information to us about what is going on inside of them. When we register this information, our brain actually treats it as an experience shared with them (Iacoboni, 2008). This means that when we see our clients' discomfort, we will feel as if we are struggling with them.

Here's the bottom line: You're going to become dysregulated to some degree during intense play therapy sessions. Your brain is designed to perceive threats and challenges, as we've already discovered. As a reminder, the work is not to avoid and attempt to prevent this from happening but rather to learn how to regulate through it so you can stay present and ventrally activated. In the process, you reinforce your own regulation ability as you model to children options about how they might be able to manage theirs.

MONKEY SEE, MONKEY DO

It's well understood that children learn how to regulate their own emotions by watching and perceiving their caregivers' responses. Children are able to learn through observation because of the mirror-neuron system (Iacoboni, 2007; Rizzolati, Fogassi, & Gallese, 2001). This is the "I feel what you feel" emotional empathy system. We can use it to get in sync with other people's emotions by reading facial expressions and body language and interpreting tone of voice.

When we observe an action over and over, this system also makes it possible for us to understand the actions of others and to imitate those actions (Bandura, 1977). It helps our minds make a simulated mental model of what we observe and then imitate what we've seen (Heyes, 2009). To see a great example of how this works, watch what happens in a preschool class when one of the kids yawns. Like a chain reaction, most of the other kids will yawn. Another example of the mirror-neuron system at work is when an infant attempts to stick out his tongue because he's watching Mommy or Daddy do it. Observing his parents automatically activates his mirror neurons, which prime the motor neurons, activating the tongue to stick out. This phenomenon helps explain why role modeling is such a key component of the learning process. It is speculated that in the therapeutic process, the mirror-neuron system makes it possible for the therapist and the client to share closely resonant interactions. The result is that through modeling, children are able to watch their play therapists and learn how to regulate through challenging emotions that arise during their play, which is one of the primary goals with children who are engaging in aggressive play; this is what begins to separate out working with aggression in this way from catharsis.

As we observe others, we look for the intentions behind their patterns and emotions in order to create a mental model of the others (Iacoboni, 2008). Creating these mental models is one of the major functions of the mirror-neuron system. Once we have an understanding of the intention behind the action we are observing, we are then able to imitate this action. It seems that the mirror-neuron system primes us to be able to copy others. This is why children copy the behaviors they see modeled by the adults and by other children around them.

Social psychologists Tanya Chartrand and John Bargh created an experiment where subjects were instructed to choose photos from a group of photographs. In the same room was another person pretending to also be a test subject. The real subjects were told that the experiment was to find pictures that they perceived as stimulating in some way. While the real subjects were looking through the pictures, the test subject was told to engage in a very deliberate action, such as rubbing his face or shaking his foot. Can you guess what was observed? Chartrand and Bargh found that the real subjects unconsciously began to copy the deliberate action of the test subject (Iacoboni, 2008)!

Let's translate the findings from this study to the playroom. As the child is engaging in aggressive play, the therapist begins to deliberately model regulation while feeling the dysregulation, and the child's mirror-neuron system will start to copy the strategies employed by the therapist. This is one of the ways the therapist is able to externally regulate the child. The therapist's own regulation in the intensity also works to enhance the child's nervous system's attempt at regulation. Through therapists' own mindfulness of their breath, movement, and body sensations, they are able to rock the dysregulated child and help the child return to a regulated state.

MIKEY

"You have to sit here," my 5-year-old client Mikey says as he points to a small pretend circle in the middle of the room. "It's an island, and you have to sit in it and you can't move away." These are the only words Mikey says to me. The rest of the session, he's completely silent. As I sit there on my small island in the play, my stomach starts to knot up. Realizing that if I move I will fall into the ocean, I start to feel anxious. I notice that it is hard to take a full breath. A shark puppet starts circling my island, and simultaneously I feel the anxiety well up inside me. The shark is staring at me and taunting me. My body responds with a sense of fear. My breathing becomes shallow. My body is tense. The shark jumps out of the water and lunges at me. It grabs hold of my arm with its teeth and won't let go. "A shark is biting my arm and it won't let go! I am scared!" I announce in the play.

Finally, Mikey opens the shark's mouth, releasing my arm, and the shark goes back into the water and resumes circling my small island. I notice that I am holding my breath as I wait for what is next. In the play, I can't escape. Then, once again, the shark jumps out of the water and bites me. It holds on tight with its teeth for what feels like minutes while I scream in pretend pain. Finally, Mikey again releases the shark's mouth, and I sit there in the play wondering if it is going to happen again.

MODELING REGULATION

Let's go back to the scenario of me attempting to wade into the cold Connecticut water. As the sensation of the water enters my awareness, I have to use mindfulness, breath, movement, and naming my experience out loud as ways to allow me to move toward the challenging sensations. Now let's explore each one of these techniques, how they were used with Mikey, and the effect it had on both Mikey, and me.

Mindfulness

Mindfulness means being awake. It means knowing what you are doing.
—Jon Kabat-Zinn, Wherever You Go, There You Are:
     Mindfulness Meditation in Everyday Life *(1995)*

Regulation begins with mindfulness. It begins with becoming aware of what is. This important aspect of growth is why we spend so much time as therapists engaging in reflective listening and mirroring back to our clients what we hear

them say. It's also why we track the child's play using observational statements. We are attempting to help our clients
engage in mindfulness, becoming aware of what they are
saying, doing, and feeling.

Allan Schore (1994) explains that as challenging emotional states or enactments enter the play, precipitated by
the child client, the attuned therapist uses mindfulness to
attempt to open to these internal feelings and sensations
and not move away or defend against them. The therapist is
then able to begin to modulate the intensity using authentic
dialogue describing cognitive, emotional, and sensorimotor
states, along with modeling regulation of bodily sensations
through breath and movement (Badenoch, 2008).

In the playroom, we use mindfulness to:

1. Become aware of what we are experiencing, so that
   we can effectively modulate the activation of our own
   nervous systems to stay ventrally activated and present with our clients, allowing our clients to borrow
   our regulatory capacity;

2. Feel our clients' inner world, allowing our clients to
   feel "felt" by us;

3. Become aware of our clients' nonverbal cues, allowing
   us to be more attuned with them and track for emotional flooding;

4. Become aware of our clients' play so that we can use
   reflective listening and observational statements to
   help our clients become aware of themselves;

5. Become aware of our own bodily sensations and feelings so that we can begin to sense what we need in order to open up further toward the feelings arising from the play, rather than contracting and moving away from them, thus giving the child permission to do the same;

6. Hold dual attention, allowing us to be aware of both ourselves and our clients.

I had to start with mindfulness and become aware. Once I became aware of myself and Mikey, I was then able to use breath, movement, and naming my experience (in addition to observational statements to track the play) to become the external regulator and help Mikey start to repattern his nervous system while he played out the thoughts, feelings, and body sensations related to his past traumatic memories.

Breath

Regulate the breathing, and thereby control the mind.
—B. K. S. Iyengar (1979)

The way we breathe dramatically affects our nervous systems. In fact, when we become dysregulated, so does our breathing, and vice versa. Did you know that you can create a state of dysregulation in your body simply by breathing a certain way? When you breathe shallowly (your inhalation is longer than your exhalation), you can activate your sympathetic nervous system, creating feelings of anxiety and overwhelm.

When your exhalation is longer than your inhalation for an extended period of time, on the other hand, you'll begin to feel the symptoms of hypo-arousal as your parasympathetic nervous system becomes activated. When we're in the midst of intense, aggressive play, our breathing becomes affected as our autonomic nervous system becomes activated. One of the best ways to regulate and manage the intensity we're experiencing in the playroom is through our breath.

When I first sat down on the island that Mikey had created for me, I noticed that my breathing changed. I could feel a tightening in my chest as it became harder to take a full breath. When I noticed this, I took a deep breath to allow for more air to enter my lungs. Once the shark began to circle me, the perception that I might not be safe from the shark influenced my breathing, creating the sensation of little space in my lungs as I simultaneously felt the quickening of my heart rate. My breathing became shallower. In the play when the shark bit my arm and wouldn't let go, I noticed a feeling of panic entering my body and I consciously worked toward elongating my exhale to counter the contraction. When the shark let go and returned to the water, I began to regulate myself by taking full breaths, allowing my body to discharge the energy that had just built up in the play.

As play therapists, we use breath to:

- Modulate the dysregulation in our nervous system that arises as it responds to children's initiated play and stories, allowing us to stay present and attuned;

- Modulate the intensity in children's play to support the children's ability to keep moving toward the uncomfortable thoughts, feelings, and sensations, thus becoming the external regulator;
- Model and thus encourage children to take breaths, allowing for the integration in their nervous systems of their dysregulated state;
- Activate our ventral state while simultaneously feeling the dysregulation in our bodies.

As Mikey played and activated a sympathetic response in both of us, my breath became the anchor. As I breathed, Mikey breathed. Each time he did, he rewired his breathing pattern. Mikey used my breath to help him feel safe.

Movement

The body always leads us home . . . if we can simply learn to trust sensation and stay with it long enough for it to reveal appropriate action, movement, insight, or feeling.
—Ogden, Minton, & Pain, 2006

When the goal is to teach children how to regulate through challenging emotions and sensations, it's essential for movement to be part of the therapeutic process. Without movement, the child will have a difficult time learning how to navigate the landscape in which the challenging energy arises.

As play therapists, we use movement for three reasons:

- Movement helps us become aware of what we're experiencing.
- Movement is a way to regulate our nervous systems and not get stuck in a dysregulated state.
- Our movement gives children permission to also use movement as a way to manage their internal states.

Even though I was told I had to stay on my small island and my lower body couldn't move, I could move my upper body and arms. In between the shark bites when the shark was circling the island, I took advantage of the pause in intensity in the play to allow my upper body to move and release some of the buildup. In the play, I tended to my wound by holding my arm and rubbing around the bite, modeling self-care and connection. I also rubbed and squeezed my legs to create energy flow so that the trauma energy wouldn't get stuck in the lower half of my body. And I rubbed my hand over my heart and gently rocked back and forth as a way to ground and connect with myself. The entire time I did this, Mikey watched me.

There wasn't a right way to move—I simply trusted what my body needed and followed the information, keeping in mind that whatever I chose to do needed to be within the context of the play that I was set up to experience. For example, I did not stand up and shake it out, since the point was for me to stay in a small area, feeling trapped and anxious.

I modeled regulation within the energy of the role Mikey gave me in the play.

Name Your Experience Out Loud

Of all the ways to regulate, naming your experience out loud seems to be the scariest for most play therapists. Many play therapists believe that it's not OK to name your experience out loud for fear of overwhelming the children or setting the children up to take care of the therapist. Keep in mind that what you are naming is a response to their initiated play.

I find this interesting, considering that we spend a lot of time teaching parents to do this. We teach parents about the importance of naming their emotions out loud, yet we don't do it in the playroom. In the context of parenting, we honor and encourage adults to name their experiences with an understanding that when they do so, they are modeling and teaching their children about the world of emotions. Fonagy and Target (2002) asserted that a sense of safety is created when a caregiver engages in self-reflection. Children will use the reflective function of the caretaker to become curious about their experiences (Levy, 2011). Levy, Ginott (1965), Gottman (1997), and Post (2009) also believed that so long as the expression is about the children's actions and not their characters, it is important for adults to honestly express their emotions out loud to children. Not doing this can lead to increased dysregulation and arousal for both the children and the adults (Gerhardt, 2004).

According to Daniel Siegel and Tina Bryson (2011), naming internal experiences out loud allows a person to move through painful states and helps regulate the nervous system. Siegel coined the phrase "Name it to tame it" to describe the calming effect that naming your experience out loud has on the amygdala in the brain (Siegel, 2011). Naming your experience out loud allows you to remain present with what is in your conscious awareness and move toward greater flexibility in your internal states. At the same time, according to Allan Schore (1994), blood flows to the right prefrontal cortex of the brain, a process essential to emotional regulation.

As I was playing with Mikey, I allowed myself to describe my internal experiences out loud. I said things like, "I'm scared!" and "I don't feel safe!" when the shark was circling my island. When I first sat down on my island, I said, "I'm noticing that my tummy is in a knot, and I feel anxious" and "I'm having a hard time taking a deep breath." During and after the shark attacks, I made sounds that corresponded to what it would feel like if a shark were actually biting my arm.

As play therapists, we use naming our experience out loud to:

- Provide our clients with language to describe the various emotional states and physical sensations they are setting us up to experience and are feeling inside of themselves;
- Provide our clients with permission to also name their experiences;

- Help our clients feel "felt," as verbalizing our experience helps our clients understand that we understand;
- Regulate our own nervous systems, keeping us present and ventrally activated.

As Mikey began to intensify the play, I had to connect to myself and be willing to feel and move toward the uncomfortable sensations arising in my body so that I could become the external regulator helping to modulate the intensity in the room. By staying open to my body sensations and emotions, while maintaining an understanding that I was facilitating play and not actually in danger, I was able to remain present and attuned to him. As Dan Siegel (2007) explained it, when a therapist is willing to feel what a client is feeling, the client feels felt by the therapist. It was this feeling of being felt by me, coupled with me modeling regulation, that allowed Mikey to move toward the memories, feelings, and sensations he was struggling to integrate. Consciously feeling the intensity and moving toward the heightened emotional state models to the child that it's OK to move toward the experience instead of running away from it (Siegel, 2010; Ogden, Minton, & Pain 2006; Ogden, Pain, Minton, & Fischer, 2005). The regulation also supported Mikey's ability to stay within his window of tolerance and helped the play begin to integrate rather than escalate.

He didn't learn how to manage his hyper-arousal in one session, of course, but over a few sessions he was able to move toward regulating his own nervous system. Within sessions, Mikey's breathing patterns and sensitivity to touch changed. His parents reported that he was able to talk about how he was feeling in ways he hadn't been able to do before, and that his aggressive behavior diminished significantly. His play also changed to themes of safety and nurturing as his trauma integrated.

CHAPTER 6 KEY POINTS

- One of the primary ways that children learn is through observation, by way of the mirror-neuron system. The mirror-neuron system allows the children to copy the regulatory strategies used by the therapist.
- Therapists must regulate first before they can help children regulate.
- As children play, therapists will feel the dysregulated states of the children's nervous systems, through a process called *resonance*.
- Breath, movement, and naming your experience are key elements in the regulation process and can be used to support integration of aggression in the playroom.
- Becoming mindfully aware is the first step toward regulation and integration.

The Setup

Remember always that whatsoever is happening around you is rooted in the mind. Mind is always the cause. It is the projector, and outside there are only screens—you project yourself.

—Osho (1983)

WHEN KIDS COME INTO OUR PLAYROOM, THEY SET us up to feel how they feel. Another way of saying this is that they offer us insight into their experience through their body language, words, and actions. They also do this with toys. This is truly the heart of the projective process in play therapy. As children set us up to feel how they feel, they have the opportunity to watch us manage the sensations and emotions we're holding. This fact is often overlooked and misunderstood, yet it's one of the fundamental components of being able to comprehend what the child is trying to communicate.

Children project their inner world onto the toys and therapist, setting them up to experience their perception of what it feels like to be them.

— *Synergetic Play Therapy* tenet

If a child feels anxious, you and the toys will be set up to feel anxious. If a child is struggling with rejection and not feeling good enough, you and the toys will be set up to feel rejected and not good enough. If a child is feeling overwhelmed, you and the toys will be set up to feel overwhelmed. If a child is feeling controlled, you'll be set up to feel controlled. This "Set Up" as referred to in Synergetic Play Therapy, is not a manipulative process—it is an offering of invaluable information to help us understand our clients.

Reflection

Take a moment and think about your last play therapy session. Put yourself back into the room with the child, and let yourself feel what it was like to be in relationship with the child. Ask yourself, "What was I set up to feel? What were the toys set up to feel?" Consider what was happening with your nervous system. Were you hyper-aroused? Were you hypo-aroused? Did you flip-flop back and forth? Contemplate how this information is relevant to the child's world.

Let's go back to Mikey in the last chapter. What was Mikey trying to get me to feel? As I sat there, there was an experience of anxiety and fear in my body, a sensation of being trapped and unable to protect myself in any way. My body also felt breathless in moments of the play. Let's look at how this might be relevant to Mikey's life and traumas that he was attempting to integrate. Shortly after Mikey was born, his parents realized he had a lot of tactile sensitivities. He also struggled with breathing and had frequent panic attacks as a young child. Often, these panic attacks would require hospitalization, during which he'd be held down to receive injections and have monitors placed on his body. Let's imagine what Mikey's perception of these experiences might have been. Might he have felt anxious? Terrified? In pain from the injections and the feeling of monitors on his sensitive skin? Unable to move away or protect himself? Helpless? Having a hard time breathing? Although we can't know for sure, we can speculate that this might have been his experience.

Mikey did whatever he needed to do to "set me up" to experience his perception of himself and things that have happened to him, and then he watched how I handled it. He was also spending a lot of time in his life "setting others up" to feel what was going on inside him in his attempt to integrate these feelings and sensations. The primary reason he was brought in for therapy was that he was aggressive, often scaring people in a shocking way and attempting to physically hurt them. From the perspective of the "setup," we can see that Mikey was doing everything he could to show everyone around him what he was attempting to integrate inside.

Unfortunately, everyone was shutting him down and telling him he had to stop instead of teaching and modeling to him how to handle the intensity that was arising in his hyper-aroused nervous system. They didn't understand that his aggression was an attempt at communication and regulation. It's important to note that knowing Mikey's history wasn't necessary for me to work with him this way. To do this work, we don't need to know the backstory. You will still be set up, and with what you're learning you'll be able to help your clients integrate the challenging memories and the corresponding sensations and feelings they carry inside without knowing exactly what happened.

ONE FOOT IN AND ONE FOOT OUT

There are a handful of key points that I hope to make in this book, and the concept I am about to share is one of them, so grab your highlighter or pen and star this paragraph.

Have you ever watched a movie and found yourself angry, sad, scared, hypervigilant, or all of the above within a 2-hour time frame as you watched the scenes unfolding before you? Of course you have! It is easy to become so engrossed in a movie that you feel you are actually in the movie and forget that you are watching a movie. Go one step further to realize that all of the emotions you experience while watching a movie aren't even in response to live people in front of you. You are responding to actors on a screen who also didn't actually have the events happen to them. Go even one step further to realize that what you are actually responding to is a pixilated screen with images on it. Yet I'd have a hard time convincing you that the experience in your body isn't genuine and doesn't feel *real*. The same phenomenon happens in a play therapy session. When we are in a session with the child, *intense play feels real*. This holds true whether we are active participants or we are observing the play. This is where our ventral activation needs to come in.

As Mikey set me up through his play to experience his perception of himself and the events in his life that he was working through, I knew that it wasn't really happening to me. I knew that I wasn't really on a small island being attacked by a shark, even though my body didn't know it. This is a key understanding in this book.

We have to be in it and not in it, simultaneously. What this means is that we have to allow ourselves to feel the realness of the dysregulation in our bodies that will naturally arise as we are in and observing the play, while knowing that it is the child's play. Teresa Kestly (2014) described it as the ability to track the felt sense (right hemisphere) and conscious awareness (left hemisphere) simultaneously. The tracking of both of these experiences is how we maintain a neuroception of safety, which allows us to stay regulated and present. When we don't hold this dual awareness, we risk either moving too far away from our clients or merging with them. The use of mindfulness, breath, moving, and naming your experience all support your ability to keep one foot in and one foot out.

I ask my students to think of "one foot in and one foot out" as a mantra they can take into the playroom as a reminder to feel it, but not get lost in it.

Here are some clues in the playroom letting you know when you have one foot in and one foot out.

- You can still track time. You know how much time you have left at any point in the session.
- You are aware of what is going on around you and are not lost in the child's play.
- You know that you are safe, even when aggression arises and the play becomes intense.
- You are aware of your body—you are tracking your breathing and can notice the sensations inside of you.
- You are aware of the child and can track the child's nonverbal cues while noticing the activation and regulation in the child's body.
- You don't take the play personally.
- You can feel the emotions arising in the child's play but aren't consumed by them.
- You don't try to rescue the child out of discomfort.
- You have a feeling of being "with" the child but also recognize that you are separate from the child.

IS IT ME OR IS IT YOU?

When we look at others, we find both them and ourselves.
—*Iacoboni (2007, p. 139)*

"How do I know that what I am feeling isn't just mine?" and "How do I separate out my experience from the child's experience?" are two of the most common questions I hear regarding the projective process.

Let's take a look at another aspect of the mirror-neuron system a bit more to understand what is happening between two people. The discovery of these neurons in the 1980s by Giacomo Rizzolatti, Giuseppe Di Pellegrino, Luciano Fadiga, Leonardo Fogassi, and Vittorio Gallese at the University of Parma really began to help us understand that the experiences we have when we are in relationship with others is a shared experience. In fact, you can't really separate out the two. Dan Zahavi (2001) stated that two people's experiences "reciprocally illuminate one another and can only be understood in their interconnection." Iacoboni went so far to state, "We cannot and should not artificially separate self and other (2008, p. 133). What this practically means is that "in other people, we see ourselves" (p. 134).

Imagine this for a minute. Wherever you are as you read this, all of a sudden, a woman walks in the room. You immediately orient to her and, consciously or not, you register her facial expression and the energy in her body. The person you are observing is moving quickly toward you, her eyes are opened wide, and her energy is frenetic. How do you feel as you imagine this? Most likely, if you are attuned to your body, you will notice that you are feeling a bit anxious. The question is, whose anxiety is it? Are you feeling yours, or are you feeling the person's? The answer is both.

It turns out that as we observe others, our brains create a full simulation—even the motor components—of what we are observing. It is as if for a moment we imagine being the person we are observing. Our brain actually attempts to feel what the other person is experiencing, and it treats what we observe as an experience shared with others (Iacoboni, 2008).

As Iacoboni wrote,

> Our mirror neurons fire when we see others expressing their emotions, as if we were making those facial expressions ourselves. By means of this firing, the neurons also send signals to emotional brain centers in the limbic system to make us feel what other people feel. (p. 119)

Let's pause for a minute to discuss the relevance of this in the playroom and weave together what we have learned so far. When children are engaging us in dramatic play or asking us to observe play that they are creating, we are picking up on the children's nonverbal and verbal cues. These cues we are picking up on are the various states of activation of the children's autonomic nervous systems. As children play and the challenging thoughts, feelings, and sensations arise inside of them, their autonomic nervous systems will simultaneously activate. You will begin to see signs of sympathetic activation or dorsal parasympathetic activation in the children. As you observe the children, you will experience somatic shifts within yourself. This happens automatically, whether we want it to or not, and is why the play feels so real in our bodies.

Marco Iacoboni (2008) wrote,

Mirror neurons provide an unreflective, automatic simulation (or "inner imitation" . . .) of the facial expressions
of other people, and this process of simulation does not
require explicit, deliberate recognition of the expression
mimicked. Simultaneously, mirror neurons send signals to
the emotional centers located in the limbic system of the
brain. The neural activity in the limbic system triggered
by these signals from mirror neurons allows us to feel
the emotions associated with the observed facial expressions. . . . Only after we feel these emotions internally are
we able to explicitly recognize them. (p. 112)

One of the biggest paradigm shifts we need to make as
play therapists is the realization that we can't avoid transference and countertransference in the playroom. I would even
argue that this is the only thing going on—transference and
countertransference is the therapeutic landscape. Therapy
is a shared experience between the clinician and the client,
and both get activated (Bullard, 2015).

We have become so afraid of our own activation, thinking that somehow it will harm the child, that we've missed
what neuroscience is now revealing: The activation is an
unavoidable shared experience. It is time we stop avoiding
what we can't prevent from happening and instead learn to
use it.

CHAPTER 7 KEY POINTS

- Children come into the playroom and through their words, actions, and play set the therapist and the toys up to feel how they feel.
- The concept of "one foot in and one foot out" means allowing yourself to feel the realness of the play while simultaneously knowing it is play. This is crucial for maintaining a neuroception of safety in the midst of the dysregulation that arises in the play.
- Whether you are an active participant or observer, "the setup" feels real.
- All experiences are shared experiences—our brain attempts to feel what the other person is experiencing and treats that experience as if it were our own.
- Transference and countertransference cannot be avoided in the playroom.

Authentic Expression

"THERE IS A GHOST BEHIND YOU!" JACK SHOUTED.

"I'm scared! I'm scared!" I said, putting my right hand on my heart and the other hand on my stomach. I exhaled loudly in an attempt to ground myself.

"And one over there, and another one there," he said, pointing to the corner of the room. "They're gonna hurt you!" he exclaimed.

"I'm so scared. I don't feel safe. I don't have any protection," I said, while continuing to breathe and hold on to myself.

Jack rolled his blue eyes. "Whatever. We're just playing."

Jack came to me because his parents were concerned about his high levels of aggression and what they referred to as his "irrational fears." During the intake with his mother, it was obvious that she was frustrated with him and emotionally disconnected from herself. When I asked her how she felt about his anger and fears, she looked at me and bluntly said, "I don't do anger." She then went on to share that his obsession with ghosts was just too much for her.

In our first play therapy session together after Jack intro-duced the ghosts to the play, he told me there were bad guys in the hallway that might enter the room at any second, and he would try to shut me down when I acknowledged the fear he was attempting to have me name. Jack used his play to set me up to understand his overwhelming sense of fear along with a clear message that it wasn't OK for him to express his feelings. At 5 years old, Jack had internalized the mes-sages he heard around him about his anger and fear and was already learning how to emotionally shut down.

As he played, I allowed myself to feel and express an authentic response based on how I would actually feel if there were ghosts in the room and bad guys in the hallway. I also allowed myself to regulate throughout the hyper-arousal, because the hypervigilance in his play was intense! Each time I expressed my fear, I noticed that I was placing one hand on my heart and the other on my stomach. I hadn't planned to do that. It was my body's natural response. When the fear in his play was named, Jack made fun of me while simultaneously trying to scare me. He'd mock me, saying things like, "I'm never scared. I'm not scared of anything." Yet he placed every toy gun, sword, shield, grenade, and even a pair of handcuffs in front of the door just in case the bad guys got in.

Two sessions later, Jack and I were playing in the sand

tray, and I saw him hide a plastic snake under the sand behind a boy figurine. As he began to move the snake through the sand to scare the boy, I felt the fear rise up inside me, and once again I allowed myself to have an authentic reaction.

"There's that feeling inside me again," I whispered hesitantly. "I feel scared, but I'm worried I can't say it because I might get told I'm not allowed to be scared."

Jack looked at me and stood up straight. "I get scared," he announced. This was the first time he'd acknowledged his fear and not made fun of me.

I felt my body relax, and I could feel the significance of the moment. I took a deep breath to hold the space for him. "You do?"

"Yes. I even know what to do when I get scared."

"What do you do?" I asked, breathing deeply to hold this poignant moment.

"Watch," he said, as he put one hand on his heart and the other on his stomach and let out a long breath. I'd never told Jack to stop and take a deep breath when he was scared. He had seen me do it and learned by watching me. My willingness to respond authentically and move toward the uncomfortable emotions allowed him to learn a coping strategy to regulate his nervous system. He knew I was being real and was in tune with him, which allowed him to begin to move toward the emotions that he had already started to shut down inside of him. By working with Jack in this way, I was helping him to change synaptic connections by engaging his mirror-neuron system. As he observed me modeling self-regulation in the midst of an intense emotion, he learned that he didn't have to deny his own emotions and sensations but rather could embrace them and learn how to regulate through them. He learned not only that it was OK to feel scared but that he would be OK if he allowed himself to fully feel it, too.

CAN I REALLY BE ME?

When we talk about authenticity, we tend to think, "Well, of course we've got to be authentic with the child." But I've found that there is some resistance to being ourselves in relationship with our child clients. I can't tell you how many times I've heard play therapists say, "I can't say that to a child" or "I can't do that!" We get so worried about emotionally hurting children or putting them in a position where they might think they need to rescue us that we don't realize that withholding our authentic experiences potentially leaves the children feeling "missed" and "not connected" to themselves and to the therapist.

When therapists are feeling an emotion such as fear, anxiety, sadness, or anger and attempt to hide their experience, children are able to pick up on the nonverbal and verbal cues of the therapists. These cues let the children know that therapists are being inauthentic. Remember, the children's brains are looking for incongruence in the environment. Let's go one step further to realize that the therapists are actually modeling to the children what to do in those moments when those feelings arise. As an example, if therapists smile every time they are scared, change the subject, disconnect from their bodies, or pretend that they feel fine, the children learn to do the same.

I assure you that it's OK to be yourself in the playroom. In fact, it's necessary if you're going to help a child regulate through intense play, because when we're not willing to be authentic, the child will usually amp up the play to get us to have an authentic response. I have never seen a child damaged because the therapist was "real." However, I have seen children who never deeply connected to their therapists and didn't go as deep as they could have gone because their therapists were too scared to share and express their authentic experience congruently in response to the children's initiated play. I have also seen children not be able to integrate the dysregulated states of their nervous systems during aggressive play because their therapists shut down the play instead of helping the children learn how to integrate the intensity.

"SHOULDS" GET IN THE WAY

In the upcoming chapters, I'll share some practical things to do in the playroom when aggressive play or death intensifies in a hyper-aroused or hypo-aroused direction. But before I do that, it's important that we take a moment to look at all the "shoulds" and "shouldn'ts" that prevent us from being truly authentic in the playroom. I realize that being completely authentic is a radical idea for many therapists, but I can tell you firsthand that it's highly effective and necessary.

> ## Reflection
>
> Write down all the "shoulds" and "shouldn'ts" that come to mind when you think about being authentic with a child. Common examples that I hear are, "I shouldn't tell children that I'm angry," "I shouldn't tell children what I'm feeling because they might want to take care of me," and "I shouldn't be completely authentic because it might be too much for the children." After you write your list, get curious about where you learned these messages.

SHARING OUR AUTHENTIC REACTIONS

In a Synergetic Play Therapy context, *authenticity* refers to being attuned to the child and to ourselves so that we can have an authentic reaction in response to the child-initiated play. It doesn't mean sharing our personal lives or telling a child that when he handcuffed you and put you in jail, it reminded you of being punished with a time-out when you were his age. Authenticity in the playroom means being genuine and congruent about our internal states as they relate to the play that children initiate and the stories they share.

Essentially, kids are looking for two things in the intense play:

- Can the therapist hold the intensity and help them regulate through it?

- Is the therapist acting or being real?

If I'm having a robust sword fight with a child and I'm laughing or I have a big smile on my face, I'm probably not being authentic. If I'm watching aggressive play and I look scared but I'm not willing to say it out loud and I pretend I'm fine, I'm also not being authentic. If I look anxious or shut down or show other signs of being dysregulated but the words I'm saying are not congruent with my appearance, the child will pick up on my incongruence. In all these instances, I'm missing the opportunity to model how to regulate my nervous system in the midst of a challenge. I'm also giving the child a reason to increase the intensity of the play to try to get me to show up authentically, because most likely my lack of authenticity is registering as a threat to the child.

I am going to reiterate this point. Your body isn't lying. You aren't hiding anything from the child. We need to stop pretending that a child doesn't feel what is going on with us. I am going to propose that it is when we aren't willing to be honest about our experience that we risk doing harm. A real reaction provides the opportunity to work through the experience. Pretending and denying experiences does not.

It is well-known that the majority of our communication is nonverbal (Mehrabian, 1972). This means that we need to be mindful of our actions as much as our words, if not more. This is even more important with children, because they pay much more attention to what we're doing than to what we're saying. They're not listening to our words as much as they're reading us and feeling us out by watching our body language and facial expressions. They're assessing us, taking in data and determining whether we're safe or we're a threat. If something about us doesn't make sense to them, their brains will consider us a potential threat. At minimum, they will spend time trying to figure us out rather than allowing themselves to fully go into the play.

IT'S REAL TO THE CHILD, SO IT NEEDS TO FEEL REAL TO YOU

Sometimes therapists have a challenging time accessing the depth of their feelings or sensations because they're being attacked by a pool noodle or a puppet, not an actual sword or something literally dangerous. Did you know that the brain can't tell the difference between something that is actually happening to you and something you're imagining? With this in mind, remember that children are trying to set you up to feel their perception of themselves and their world, which means that whatever is happening feels real to them. So it needs to feel real to you in order to access the authentic response they're looking for.

This is a very important point to understand. I tell my students to imagine, just for a moment, that whatever is happening to them or whatever they're witnessing is real. I ask them to respond as if it were really happening. The moment they do, out comes an authentic response that's congruent with the energy in the room. The risk of not doing this is that children will continue to amp it up until you eventually have an authentic response that mirrors the feelings in their inner world, or they will give up.

Let's explore this a little deeper. You might be wondering, "But aren't I being authentic if I'm really not scared by a pool noodle or a puppet? Isn't expressing fear, when I know it's a puppet and isn't really going to hurt me, being inauthentic?" And the answer is yes and no. What I find with scenarios like this is that therapists are either focusing on the nonthreatening toy itself instead of feeling the energy that's arising because of the way the child is using the toy, or they are in their heads, not allowing themselves to feel. The trick is to have both experiences so that you don't emotionally flood or get absorbed by the experience but are still able to be present in the intensity. Remember, you have to be in the experience, feeling the sensations and emotions that arise (dysregulation), while simultaneously having the awareness that you're not really in danger (ventral activation). Use mindfulness and regulation to help you. If you believe you really are in danger or you're about to leave your window of tolerance, it's time to set a boundary.

This same concept is true for role-playing. Role-playing is a form of acting. When we're being scolded and thrown in the dungeon in the play, unless we allow ourselves to imagine that the play is real and respond accordingly, we will be faking our responses. The child will know we're not being authentic. The more we can allow our minds to embrace what the setup would feel like if it were really happening, the more authentic our responses will be and the more congruent they will be in the eyes of the child we are playing with.

CHANGING THE NEURAL PATHWAYS

In Synergetic Play Therapy, therapists try to be as authentic and congruent as possible during the play session. In doing so, we transmit the trust and safety our clients need for healing from the intensity of their traumatic experiences. The therapist's authenticity helps maximize attunement, allowing the therapist to serve as an external regulator for the client's dysregulated state (Schore, 1994). In other words, when we're being authentic, we can play a critical role in teaching kids how to regulate their nervous systems and change their brain activity (Dion & Gray, 2014). As Badenoch (2008) and Siegel (1999) explained, when the child's mirror-neuron system is activated, the therapist's mindfulness and authentic expression can trigger new brain activity that can become associated with the feelings in the neural nets of memories.

When children repeatedly see us being authentic and present in the midst of the activation of the dysregulated states of the nervous system, their old programming can be interrupted, creating an opening for a new experience and giving them permission to move toward challenging internal states the way they see us do it. As children move toward their challenging internal states, new neural connections can be created and eventually initiate new neural organization (Edelman, 1987; Tyson, 2002; Dion & Gray,

2014). We now know that with dedicated amounts of repetition, neural systems can change; however, we also know that most therapeutic interventions don't achieve that goal (Perry, 2006).

When Jack brought the feelings of anxiety and fear to life in the playroom, he witnessed me repeatedly putting my hand on my chest and my stomach for self-care while simultaneously taking a deep breath. Within only a few sessions, he was able to move toward the intensity and eventually try the self-regulation behaviors modeled for him. It required a commitment from me to be authentic for this to occur. I stayed as authentic as I could in the midst of his making fun of me, trying to shut me down, and doing everything he could to scare me. I understood that everything occurring was part of the setup, and that my job was to help him feel "felt" and to help him integrate the intensity while offering options for self-regulation through modeling. The result was that Jack was able to create new neural connections that resulted in a new neural organization. What's thrilling is that when we work with kids this way, every session has the potential to help them integrate new information and rewire past encoded experiences (Schore, 1994; Siegel, 1999; Badenoch, 2008).

CHAPTER 8 KEY POINTS

- When children perceive their therapist as incongruent, they will often amp up the play until the therapist has an authentic and congruent response. Authenticity helps create safety.

- Having a genuine, authentic response to the child's initiated play and stories is not role-playing.
- When therapists are not willing to be authentic in the playroom, their incongruence registers as a potential threat in the child's brain.
- The play feels real to the children, so it needs to feel real to you in order to have the authentic and congruent response they are seeking.
- As children see a therapist authentically modeling regulation, they learn that it is safe to move toward the uncomfortable thoughts, feelings, and sensations inside. As they do this, they begin to change the neural pathways in their brain toward a higher regulatory capacity, allowing for integration.

Setting Boundaries

SARAH, AGE 6, WALKED OVER TO THE TOY SHELF and quickly spotted the handcuffs. She picked them up and closely examined the lock, as if attempting to discover whether they'd do the job. When she turned around and looked directly at her therapist, his eyes widened and his breathing changed. He was visibly anxious. She ran toward him, grabbed his arm, and tried to force it behind his back, but he pulled his arm away from her.

"We can't do that in here," he said. "It's not OK to handcuff me."

Sarah was stunned. Her body language and facial expression spoke volumes. She thought she'd done something terribly wrong.

I saw this exchange during a play therapy session observation. I'm sharing this story to shed light on new possibilities. We've all set boundaries out of fear or frustration and then questioned whether the boundary was actually necessary or regretted the way we'd gone about it. Setting bound-aries is an extremely important topic in play therapy. There are many beliefs and ideas about how to do it, when to do it, and even why a therapist needs to do it, so in order to create clarity on this subject, we have to stop and ask ourselves this important question: What is the point of the boundary?

I've asked my students this question hundreds of times, and inevitably their responses are something like, "I don't know. Isn't that what I'm supposed to do?" or "The child can't act like that in the session. I have to teach her appro-priate ways to behave" or "It's not OK for me or my toys to be treated that way."

Before we explore a new way of understanding and work-ing with boundaries, answer the following question.

Reflection

Take a moment and think about why you set boundaries in the playroom. (It might help to think of a child you have set a boundary with and answer the question with that child in mind.) Take another moment to write your answers down.

Your answers are not right or wrong. What you've writ-ten is information about your beliefs and your window of tolerance. As you read this chapter, I encourage you to reflect on your answers. When you finish the chapter, read your written response and see if you'd like to revise or add to it in any way.

BOUNDARIES ARE PERSONAL!

What I'm about to introduce might conflict with other ideas you've heard about setting boundaries. If you find yourself shaking your head, furrowing your brow, or pursing your lips, that's great! As play therapists, it's important for us to question our thinking and be open to shifting our paradigms regarding what "should" or "shouldn't" happen in a play therapy session.

Reflection

Look at the answers you just wrote down. How much of them are based on a "should" or a belief about what is appropriate behavior?

Therapists can find themselves struggling with an internal conflict the moment they think a boundary might be necessary. If a boundary is set because we think we're "supposed to" or "should" set one, we might not feel confident about our decision and may question ourselves afterward. Remember that "shoulds" are felt as a threat to the self and get in the way of authenticity!

Sometimes therapists set boundaries because they truly believe the boundary is necessary to teach a child about appropriate behavior, but then they feel a bit disconnected from the child or wonder why the child escalated or pulled back, like in the story at the beginning of this chapter.

I'm sharing these examples not to judge what was good or bad but because they have information that can help us. When we become clear about why we're setting the boundary, we can do it in a way that doesn't cause the child or ourselves to feel shame.

BOUNDARIES ARE IMPORTANT!

When setting a boundary, it's important that you still get to be yourself, and so does the child. We can achieve this if we shift our rationale for why we're setting the boundaries in the first place.

Are you ready for the new paradigm? Take a deep breath, move your body as you read this, and regulate so that you can take this in.

Kids don't need boundaries in the playroom—therapists do!

Let's review the purpose of aggression in the playroom. A play therapy session is where children get to learn how to regulate their nervous systems and integrate all the challenging memories, emotions, and body sensations that arise as they attempt to play out and understand their perceptions of themselves and their lives, including aggression.

It's important that we don't shut down children's need to express whatever they're trying to express.

Our job is to help children find a way to keep the energy moving. This doesn't mean that therapists are punching bags or that we allow whatever happens to happen. The difference in the paradigm is that the boundary is for the therapist. The moment we think that if children continue doing whatever they are doing, we will have a hard time staying present or become dysregulated to the point of getting flooded, it's time to set a boundary!

Boundaries are necessary for keeping us in our window of tolerance, allowing us to stay present and attuned. Our window of tolerance is the container that holds the energy that's emerging from the aggressive play. Many students have asked me, "When should I set the boundary?" And my answer is, "I have no idea. How can I know when you need it or how big your window of tolerance is in a particular moment?" Only you know when you need to set a boundary.

SETTING BOUNDARIES IS A FLEXIBLE EXPERIENCE

There are days that my window of tolerance is really big, and so is my capacity to stay present in the intensity. There are other days when I don't feel well or something has occurred in my personal life that influences my energy and level of presence. Staying present on some days is definitely easier than it is on others, and I think we need to be honest with ourselves about that.

Our personal history might also be a factor in when we need to set a boundary. If therapists were hit as children or witnessed violence, and the emotions of those experiences are not fully integrated, it could be more challenging for them to stay present if the child wants them to witness violent fighting with the toys or to be in the play itself. The time for therapists to set a boundary is the moment they get a sense that the play is too much for their nervous systems to hold.

We also have physical limitations that can influence when we need to set a boundary. During a play therapy session I had with a young boy while I was pregnant, he wanted to handcuff me to the door so that I'd have to swordfight with one hand and not be able to move around. I knew I wouldn't be able to protect my baby if he swung at my stomach, and I wouldn't be able to focus on the sword fight knowing that my baby wasn't safe, so that was a time for me to set a boundary.

There are many reasons why a boundary might be necessary, and most are related to helping the therapist stay present.

HOW TO SET BOUNDARIES

Based on this new paradigm, we set boundaries to help us create a neuroception of safety, allowing us to engage our ventral state, be present, and step in as the external regulator. We set the boundaries the moment we can't stay in our own window of tolerance for whatever reason. So how do we do it? What does setting a boundary look like?

First, we want to keep in mind that we're not trying to stop the energy (this is what our fear response wants us to do). We're trying to redirect it in such a way that allows us to stay present and continues to allow the child to explore the emotions and sensations that are arising. We want to keep them engaged in the play without triggering their brains' perception of us as a threat.

Let's explore a few scenarios and discuss them from the child's perspective.

Scenario 1

In the story of Sarah and her therapist at the beginning of this chapter, when the therapist stopped the play and told Sarah it wasn't OK to handcuff him, Sarah stopped and was confused. Why?

Sarah's brain most likely experienced two things: incongruence in the environment and a "should," or in this case a "shouldn't." Her brain might have been thinking, "If there are handcuffs in here, why wouldn't I be allowed to put them on you? Isn't that what they're for? If not, why are they in here?"

Scenario 2

You're engaged in an intense moment of play with 4-year-old Ben and he's shouting, stabbing at you, and coming at you from every direction. Suddenly, you know you've had it. "OK, you know what? That's too much," you say. "We can't play like that in here."

Ben's brain has a high probability of registering this as a threat because of the confusion and the abrupt nature of the boundary setting. Ben is stopped in the middle of his expression and given the message that his expression is not OK. He will probably experience an internal conflict between what his nervous system needs to do and what he's told he can't do. In all probability, this is the same message he gets outside the playroom when he becomes hyper-aroused and sets others up to feel overwhelmed.

Scenario 3

You're sword fighting with 9-year-old Sally, and she catches you off guard and hits you pretty hard. Your buttons get pushed and you say sternly, "So, there's a rule in here that therapists aren't for hurting. You can't hurt me."

Sally's brain will most likely register this as a threat because she's receiving a "shouldn't" message. She might also be confused by the incongruence of the therapist's engaging in a sword fight but then saying that therapists aren't for hurting. People sometimes get hurt in sword fights.

Another consideration is that when therapists set rules like "You can't hurt me" in the context of trauma work, they're inadvertently telling children that in that moment, they are perpetrators. The therapist has just made the child the bad guy in the room and turned the aggression into a personal experience, rather than remembering that this is all part of the setup and finding another way to set the boundary.

When setting boundaries based on a "should" or a "shouldn't" or out of fear, consider that the child has probably experienced some version of this in life and may still be experiencing it. Children try to express their hyper-aroused state and most likely get feedback such as "Stop. Contain. Calm down. You're too much." Consider the possibility that when we abruptly stop the play and say no, what we're doing is reinforcing that it isn't OK to express certain feelings and reinforcing the brain wiring that supports that story, too.

It's not uncommon for children to amp it up when they feel shamed, controlled, or threatened by a boundary. I've witnessed countless interactions where, as soon as the therapist sets a boundary, children do everything they can to regain a sense of control over the therapist. In a nutshell, children will set therapists up to feel what having the boundary set just felt like to them.

KEEPING THE FLOW: ACKNOWLEDGE AND REDIRECT

As you set boundaries, the following are important:

- Take a deep breath to ground yourself.
- Get present so that the child can energetically feel you.

- When you speak, use a nonthreatening yet serious voice.
- Make eye contact when possible, but don't force it.
- Acknowledge before redirecting.
- Keep your feelings out of it!

Now let's explore a few examples of how to set boundaries without saying no or stopping the play, while keeping the energy moving and staying connected to the child.

Redirect With Actions

Help children understand where they can direct their energy that is within your window of tolerance. In a sense, you are telling the children what they can do instead of what they can't do.

Example 1: *Gesture where you want the energy to go*

You're having a fast-paced sword fight with 6-year-old Shawn, and he's swinging at your head, and you're starting to feel overwhelmed. It's just too much, and you don't think you can stay present much longer if he keeps swinging at your head. As you're fighting, you look him in the eye, change your voice, and say, "Shawn, hit me from here down," as you gesture toward everything below your head.

Example 2: *Bring in containment to keep it moving*

For 20 minutes, 8-year-old Janet plays out various scenes in the sand tray, all extremely violent in some way. You have a history of witnessing violence as a child, and you start to notice that inside you are feeling quite anxious and are beginning to move toward the end of your window of tolerance. Janet then begins to attempt to dump all the sand out of the sand tray onto the floor. Since you are already close to your limit, you feel a strong need to control and stop her arise in your body, signaling to you that it's time to set a boundary. You make eye contact with her and, changing your voice so that it's different from the voice you've been using, say, "Janet, this is so important for you to do. The sand needs to come out." You grab a shower curtain and quickly put it on the floor and invite her to continue dumping the sand onto the shower curtain. You are once again able to be present and help facilitate her process. (Had she not organically shifted her play to the sand and the violence in the play continued, the therapist could have instructed her, "Show me another way," as described below.)

Redirect With Words

Sometimes saying less is better than saying more. Here are two go-to phrases that are incredibly powerful to use in the playroom. I call them the "golden statements" in boundary setting. With both phrases, it is important that they are said as statements and not asked as questions.

Example 1: *"Show me another way"*

Tyler, age 3, grabs a scoop of sand and lunges toward you, trying to put sand in your mouth and eyes.

You look Tyler in the eye and, changing your voice, say, "Show me another way."

Tyler says, "No. In mouth."

You look him in the eye again, get present, and say, "Tyler, this is so important to you. You need the sand to go on a face and in a mouth. Show me with a different face and mouth." (You'd have to get more specific, since he's 3 and in the midst of enacting a trauma memory.)

He walks to the shelf and grabs a baby doll, puts her on the floor, and proceeds to pour the sand into her eyes and mouth.

Example 2: *"I don't need to hurt to understand"*

After Julie, age 6, unexpectedly throws markers at you, hitting you for the second time after you've attempted twice to acknowledge and redirect her play, you take a deep breath, look at her, and say, "Julie, I don't have to hurt to understand." You follow it up with, "Show me another way."

She looks at you while once again reaching for the markers.

You make eye contact with her, ground yourself, and using a nonthreatening but serious voice, you say again, "I don't need to hurt to understand." You take another deep breath, and this time she puts the marker down.

Children really need to know that you understand and that you're not trying to control or stop the play. Most important, they need to feel you and your respect. Setting boundaries in these ways in the midst of the play teaches children about listening, empathy, and respecting the needs of another. The message the therapist is delivering is "Let's meet in the middle, and I'm going to take care of myself " rather than "You have to stop because I'm uncomfortable." What a beautiful lesson in relationship to have modeled to the child.

In all of these examples, the children felt understood. They also felt respected, which is very important. The majority of children will shift and find another way when the boundary is set in this way, because the truth is that they want to play with you and they want you to understand. When you're able to stay regulated and in attunement with the child as you set the boundary, you allow the child's nervous system to continue to do what it needs to do. There will be a few children who won't redirect their play right away, and you might have to say it a few times. This is OK. Check in to make sure you are including the tips I mentioned above, and just keep acknowledging and redirecting.

AM I ENCOURAGING AGGRESSION?

The fear of encouraging aggression is the most common fear that comes up when I teach this new perspective. Therapists fear that if they don't set a boundary when they think they "should," the child will become more aggressive at home or at school. Therapists are afraid that they'll somehow promote the aggressive behavior. What I've found, however, is that when therapists are authentically using mindfulness, movement, and breath and naming their experience out loud to regulate the intensity in the room, in addition to making observational statements about the child's play, it allows children to explore their highly activated dysregulated states and they begin to develop a sense of awareness regarding their urges, sensations, intensity, and emotions. As the children move toward their intensity in a more mindful way, the intensity actually begins to dissipate as they become more present and connected with themselves. Rarely does the child become more aggressive at home or at school, but when this does happen, there's usually something else going on in the environment that the child is continuing to perceive as a high threat or challenge.

On the other hand, when therapists act or role-play, don't name their authentic experience while regulating the intensity, or just use observational statements, children typically amp up the play until they get an authentic response. Although there's a discharge and catharsis, it doesn't necessarily mean that the energy is being integrated or that the children are developing a strong sense of awareness of their sensations and emotions. This is what leads to the potential for more acting-out behaviors outside the therapy sessions. Don't underestimate the power of your authentic presence and your role as the child's external regulator.

SAFETY CONCERNS

Are you ready for another truth moment? Whether you choose to set boundaries as I am suggesting, or choose another way, such as telling children that they can't do whatever they are doing, sometimes the children are past the point of redirection, and their aggression will reach a level where either you or they could get hurt. If things escalate to the point where there are safety concerns, there is a high probability that you will have to set a strong boundary and possibly even use the word *no*. My experience is that these moments are rare, but they happen nonetheless.

Have you ever been around people while they are having a seizure? If so, you know that when people are in the middle of a seizure, you don't touch them other than to put something under their head or to hold their head to keep it safe. You let the energy of the seizure move through. Your job is to get out of the way and to keep them safe in their environment. When a child has hit this level of aggression, it is a similar process. Your primary job is to keep yourself and the child safe, and you will need to get creative and trust your intuition to feel your way through the experience. There isn't a guidebook for these moments. It is, however, probably not the time to try and engage the child in a rational process. It is often best in these moments to stop talking and to breathe. Get grounded and present, so that the child can feel you. Here is the honest truth about these moments: You do the best you can, knowing that it is going to be emotionally messy and that repair will likely need to happen.

THE REPAIR

Sometimes, doing what you can to regulate the intensity in the play will not be enough. It's inevitable that even after practicing what you learn in this book, you'll have a session that's so intense and overwhelming that you'll forget to set a boundary; you will go past your own window of tolerance and become highly dysregulated. You're human, remember. In other words, you will emotionally flood. In these moments, you'll most likely then set a boundary out of fear, and it will register in the child's mind as abrupt, controlling, and possibly even shaming. If and when this happens, know that you're not the only one. I have yet to meet a play therapist who hasn't done this. The beautiful part about this is that when we have a very human moment, we get to do the repair. I love repairs because the modeling that occurs for a child is so profound and priceless.

> ### Reflection
>
> Take a moment and imagine or recall setting a boundary out of fear and becoming angry and stern with a child. What was happening? What might you try differently next time if the same situation were to happen again?

As soon as you realize that you set your boundary out of fear and that you didn't quite handle it the way you wanted to, you have a chance to do repair work right away in the session or at the next session. For example, at the beginning of your next session with the child, imagine saying something like, "Joey, remember last time when we were playing and I got mad all of a sudden and told you to stop and that it wasn't OK to play like that? I realized that my brain got really scared and that's why I said what I said. I also realized that I didn't do enough things to take care of myself, like breathing, moving, and telling you how I was feeling, so when I got scared, I got scared fast! What I really wanted to say but couldn't find the words was 'Show me another way.' So if you decide today that you would like to play like that again and I need to take care of myself, this time I will just ask you to show me another way so that we can keep playing. Playing with you is really important to me."

What does this teach the child?

- It's OK to be human.
- When we do something that we know affects another person, we take responsibility.
- It's important to try again.

As your window of tolerance expands, you'll probably feel comfortable setting fewer boundaries, and the types of boundaries you'll need will tend to change. The majority of the time, when children become aggressive, they will still be able to be redirected without the word *no*, without being told that what they are doing is not OK, and without having their play shut down. It is important that we work to set boundaries in such a way that doesn't shame a child and that allows for the process to keep moving.

CHAPTER 9 KEY POINTS

- Boundaries are used to help therapists stay within their window of tolerance, so that they can continue to hold and regulate the intensity, supporting the child's integration.
- When setting boundaries, it is important to keep the energy moving without shutting the play down. It is also important to acknowledge and redirect instead of using the word *no* whenever possible.
- "Show me another way" and "I don't need to hurt to understand" are golden statements in boundary setting.
- When there are physical safety issues involved, it is important to set a boundary.
- When setting boundaries doesn't go well, having a reparative moment with the child is deeply therapeutic.

It Is Too Intense: Working With Emotional Flooding

MAX, AGE 10, WAS PRETEND SHOOTING MOLLY IN their play. He had her backed into a corner. She stopped the play and told him that it wasn't OK for him to point the gun at her. He didn't listen and started to shoot her. She told him again that it wasn't OK, and he escalated. He started to yell at her and wouldn't stop pretend shooting. Feeling overwhelmed and not knowing what to do, Molly tried to grab the gun away from Max to get him to stop. He bit her hand. She then told him that it wasn't OK to bite her. He bit her again and then tried to kick her. All of this was happening while he was still trying to pretend shoot her and emotionally escalating.

Although we may wish this were just a really bad scene from a movie, we know that it wasn't. This was a play therapy session, and moments like this happen in our profession more often than we would like to admit. This particular situation was presented to me during a consultation. The therapist was filled with so much shame and confusion regarding what had happened and how she'd handled it. "Why didn't he listen to me?" she kept asking me. There are many parts to her answer, but a main reason was because they were both emotionally flooded.

UNDERSTANDING EMOTIONAL FLOODING

The more I learn about the brain and body's capacity for regulation, the more I am in awe of it. The brain and its corresponding nervous system's ability to do exactly what it needs to do when faced with perceived challenges and intensity is truly extraordinary.

Our window of tolerance changes from moment to moment. When we are in our window of tolerance, we are able to manage the thoughts, feelings, and sensations that we experience. When we are outside of our window of tolerance, we begin to move toward the experience of emotional flooding. Think of it like water filling a cup. The cup has reached its capacity and can no longer hold the water, and the water is now overflowing. In these moments, our brains have registered the data coming in as too much and too fast, as in my story at the beginning of this book and the story at the beginning of this chapter. When this happens, our nervous systems respond in two ways—excessive sympathetic activation and dorsal activation.

The content in this book is guiding you toward a greater ability to notice when you are beginning to move outside of your window of tolerance, approaching emotional flooding, as well as how to recognize these symptoms in your child clients. It is also showing you ways to stay within your window of tolerance so that you can support children in learning how to stay in theirs.

EMOTIONAL FLOODING IS PART OF RELATIONSHIP

Emotional flooding happens in every play therapy model because emotional flooding is part of relationship.

No one is immune to the experience of emotional flooding, and no play therapy theory or technique is either. It occurs in both directive and nondirective approaches. I have yet to meet a play therapist who has not experienced emotional flooding or been with a child when the child also emotionally flooded in the playroom.

Understanding emotional flooding and what to do when it is starting to happen is truly one of the most important parts of learning how to work with intensity in the playroom. During emotional flooding, the probability of the therapist and child getting hurt increases, either physically or emotionally, which is why it is necessary to talk openly and honestly about it.

WHAT DOES FLOODING LOOK LIKE?

There are two ways that our bodies respond to "too much" data coming in. One way is through sympathetic activation (escalation), and the other way is through dorsal parasympathetic activation (shutdown or collapse). Since the focus of this book is aggression, I am choosing to highlight and discuss emotional flooding as it relates to sympathetic activation. Although I am emphasizing sympathetic flooding, it is also extremely important to know that when a child begins to shut down and energetically collapse, these are signs of emotional flooding with dorsal activation.

Have you ever been around a child who started to rapidly escalate? Sometimes I refer to this as the child reaching "the point of no return." This is that moment when children are so sympathetically aroused that they fly off the handle, and they can no longer hear you or even see you. They are escalating like a train with a faulty break system gaining speed, and you know that the only way it is going to stop is when it crashes into something. Of course you've seen this. You can also most likely recall a time in your life when you *were* this train.

Maybe the child was in a full rage in your playroom; or trying to climb your shelves and throw the toys off; or running around your office trying to escape, break, or dump things. Maybe the child was even trying to hit you, bite you, or throw something at you. These are examples of sympathetically aroused emotional flooding.

In the situation with Max and Molly described at the beginning of this chapter, Max eventually reached a point where he was so emotionally flooded that he could no longer manage his internal experience. At this point, he started to bite and hit Molly. Molly, also overwhelmed by the experience, was not regulating to stay connected to herself and ground the intensity, so she also started to emotionally flood. She was setting boundaries in a way that Max couldn't hear and most likely felt threatened by. As she became scared, she responded with aggression and an attempt to control Max. His behavior escalated.

WORKING WITH EMOTIONAL FLOODING

I have described how even with the best of intentions, there will be times when flooding is going to happen.

Once children have emotionally flooded, there is only one task at hand: to create a neuroception of safety and help the children return into their window of tolerance. When a brain becomes emotionally flooded, the parts of the brain that can think rationally are temporarily out of service, and their ability to self-govern quickly diminishes. Attempting to engage children in a discussion about what is happening inside of them or about their behavior will most likely escalate the situation.

There is no script for these moments. These moments require your presence, your own ability to regulate, your creativity, and your intuition. These are the moments when the baby is screaming, and you as the attuned caregiver have to do whatever it takes to help the baby return to a regulated state. These moments require your ability to hold the intensity. These moments require you to move toward the intensity and not run away. They require a commitment to stay connected to yourself, so that you can attune to each moment and to do what is needed to rock the baby.

Morgan, age 8, came to see me because of the aggressive outbursts she was having at school, sometimes striking out at her peers and her teachers.

During the play, she decided to create a scenario with a toy horse. She grabbed a few fences and proceeded to line them up in a row, attempting to create a course for what would be equestrian jumping. As she created the course, she placed the fences incredibly close together, leaving very little space for the horse to jump and land before jumping over the next fence. As I watched this, I felt my body begin to tighten, knowing that her experience of the play was likely not going to go as planned. I knew the horse was not going to be able to fit between the fences. This was an important moment in her therapy, as she did not have a high frustration tolerance level. Moments like these in her life would often set the stage for her to hit, bolt, or abruptly quit whatever she was engaged in if she didn't feel successful at it. Rather than rescuing her from this important moment by encouraging her to change the play, I decided to become the external regulator and work with her on expanding her window of tolerance for frustration.

To do this, I began to modulate the rise of anxiety that was starting to occur in the play using my breath. Using mindfulness, I worked to stay connected to my own body in the event that she suddenly emotionally flooded. I was consciously engaging my ventral state so that I could hold her dysregulation. Once she finished setting up the scene, she grabbed a horse and started the play. She attempted to have it jump over the first fence. Just as expected, the horse couldn't fit, and it knocked two fences over. I watched her physiology carefully and noticed that her body was tensing. I could see the beginning of the sympathetic activation set in. I breathed. She then tried to make the horse jump over the next fence, and this time its foot got caught in the fence and the horse fell over. It was too much for her. She announced, "I'm done," and proceeded to stand up and walk to the door. I acknowledged the frustration and also recognized that she was flooded and was now in sympathetic flight activation. Since I had already started to regulate myself, I was able to be present with her in her flooding. I could hold what was happening, which is the integrative force that allows this to become a deeply therapeutic moment and an opportunity for repatterning.

Faster than I could stop her, she opened the door and started heading toward the waiting room. I could visibly see her arousal level. Her body was tense. Her speech was fast. Her movements had an intensity to them. I knew that my only job at that point was to help create a neuroception of safety for her so that she could return to a more regulated state.

These moments are some of the most challenging moments that can arise in therapy. They can be scary. They can be overwhelming. At minimum, they are uncomfortable. They don't often go as planned, and they often leave us with feelings of shame, guilt, and embarrassment for how we responded. They can ignite anger and blame toward the person we perceive to have created the situation. These moments have a tendency to activate our own defense responses and patterns even when we don't want them to. It is no wonder that therapists try so hard to avoid them.

IS EMOTIONAL FLOODING BAD?

Given how uncomfortable emotional flooding is, one might think that it is a bad thing for it to occur in a play therapy session. What if I told you that it wasn't? What if I told you that when it happens (because it will, no matter how hard you try for it to not happen), there is a way to make it a deeply therapeutic experience? I am here to tell you that the first step to transforming the experience of emotional flooding is to not be afraid of it happening.

Reflection

Take a moment and write down all of the fears that come up when you think about a child emotionally flooding in a session. Are you afraid that you might get hurt? Are you afraid that the child might get hurt? Are you afraid that you will lose control and not know how to set a boundary? Write them all down. Chances are, the fears that you have written down are influenced by your past experiences with emotional flooding. Consider applying the exercise on integrating a fear adapted from Dr. John Demartini, in Chapter 5, as you work toward integrating these experiences from your own history.

In the story of Morgan, I wasn't afraid that she might emotionally flood. In fact, I knew that it was likely and chose to use the experience as a moment to help her repattern. I could have easily encouraged her to move the fences apart to make room for the horse when it jumped. Instead, I chose to use the moment therapeutically, trusting that if it didn't go well, we would repair.

RUPTURE AND REPAIR CREATES SAFETY

As a field, we are so caught up in getting things "right" with our clients, and our clients not being "uncomfortable," that sometimes we exchange comfort for the opportunity for growth. Did you know that research shows that an attuned caregiver is actually only attuned 30% of the time (Tronick, 2007)? This means that even in the best-case scenario, the majority of the time relationship is actually a dance of navigating mis-attunement! When we are overly attached to the idea that a therapist must be attuned the majority of the time and things like emotional flooding should never happen, we actually miss one of the most important building blocks for creating safety in the therapeutic relationship. It is the act of having an interactive repair that strengthens emotional connection (Bullard, 2015). In fact, it is the dance that occurs between the therapist and the child as they repair the ruptures and mis-attunement that strengthens their relationship and develops trust. Rupture and repair is actually necessary to create attachment!

As I mentioned, emotional flooding is a part of relationship, and no play therapy model is immune to it occurring. This means that although we do our best to attune to our clients so that we can regulate the intensity in the playroom, sometimes mis-attunement is still going to happen. We are going to miss the cues. We are going to be distracted. Our own defense patterns will come into the session and prevent us from being able to connect to ourselves and to our clients. Sometimes the child will emotionally flood. Sometimes we will, too.

Mis-attunement provides the opportunity for rupture and repair, which creates safety in the relationship.

WHEN YOU EMOTIONALLY FLOOD

What about you in the playroom? How many times have you been so overwhelmed by what the child was doing that you checked out or started to look at the clock or started to become emotionally numb? What about becoming so angry with a child that you set a boundary out of frustration and maybe even scolded the child in some way? These are all signs of emotional flooding, and they are all normal responses to the perception of "too much."

When the therapist sympathetically emotionally floods alongside the child, it is then common that the therapist will forcefully step in to shut the play down out of the need to self-protect. This can lead to both the therapist and child feeling shame and guilt. When therapists flood in dorsal activation, they will start to shut down, numb out, and check out, resulting in an experience of disconnection that potentially leaves the child feeling "missed" or abandoned.

Tips to help the therapist from flooding:

- Get out of tunnel vision by pausing throughout the play and looking around the room. Orient yourself to the time and space.
- Remind yourself that what you are experiencing is occurring in a play therapy session—help yourself feel the play while simultaneously knowing it is just play. Tell yourself "One foot in, one foot out."
- Use your breath and movement to ground yourself.
- Name your experience out loud to help calm your amygdala.
- Make sure you are using observational statements throughout your sessions to track the play and help your rational brain stay engaged.
- Set boundaries! Acknowledge and redirect when you start to feel that the play is going outside of your window of tolerance.

As Morgan fled the room, I followed, using my breath to attune to the moment. I became the external regulator for her dysregulated state. Once we entered the waiting room, I could see that she was still flooded and in a flight response. My intuition told me that if I attempted to make her go back into the playroom, she would quickly move toward an aggressive outburst and try to hit me. In an effort to create a neuroception of safety, I looked at her and said, "It feels like a lot in here. Let's go outside." We then headed outside and started to walk around the building. As we walked, I stayed silent while using my breath and movement to ground both of us. As we were walking, we noticed that some of the trees had been cut down and had been placed in piles in the parking lot, blocking our path. When we approached the first pile, I watched her closely to see what her reaction would be, as we had just encountered another obstacle. Once again, I prepared for her to possibly emotionally flood. I could sense that she was a bit more regulated but still activated. She was right on the edge of her window of tolerance. I decided to use this moment as the opportunity to repattern her nervous system. Here is what I did: I turned the parking lot into a giant playroom. I pointed out that we were like the horses approaching the jumps each time we came closer to a pile of the cut-down trees. Together we stood in front of each pile, moving and breathing and talking about what could go wrong if we decided to jump. We regulated through the anxiety and the potential frustration. Together we figured out how to navigate the "jumps" without flooding. By the time we walked back into the building, we were holding hands and she was smiling. That experience created new neural pathways for her, and it wouldn't have happened had I rescued her out of fear of her emotional flooding. What it did require of me was to employ everything I am teaching you in this book so that I could move toward the challenge and help her regulate through it.

CHAPTER 10 KEY POINTS

- Emotional flooding happens in every play therapy model, because emotional flooding is part of relationship.
- Learning how to work with aggression the playroom requires understanding emotional flooding and what to do when it starts to happen.
- When emotional flooding occurs, the only task at hand is to create a neuroception of safety.
- Use mindfulness, breath, movement, and naming your experience out loud to help keep you from emotionally flooding.
- Safety in a relationship has a lot to do with how moments of mis-attunement/rupture and repair take place.

Observing Aggressive Play

HAVE YOU EVER WATCHED SOMETHING IN A SESSION that was highly aggressive or filled with death? Have you ever had to sit there while a child played out an intense scene that left your nervous system highly activated, in a state of hyper-arousal? Have you ever watched something so intense that you found yourself wanting to check out or numb out as hypo-arousal set in? Being set up as the observer is a common role for play therapists, either because the child sets the play up that way or because the style of play therapy being used is observational in nature.

We might have to watch a war between the army men or a scary scene set in a dollhouse where someone gets significantly hurt. We might have to watch a baby doll be thrown around the room. We might have to watch the child beat up the bop bag, puppets attack each other, or a small animal toy be shot at. It doesn't matter if you're watching or directly in the play; you're going to feel the intensity whether you consciously register it or not. Therefore, it's vitally important to practice regulating your own nervous system so that you don't walk out of your session with the symptoms of having just witnessed violence, which you did!

Observing play that is aggressive and filled with death without understanding the importance of self-regulation for yourself and for your child client is one of the fastest ways to increase the potential for burnout. It's also one of the fastest ways to create symptoms of dysregulation in your own system that stay with you long after the session is over.

Everything you've learned in this book is just as applicable when you're observing as it is when you're participating. You're still working toward authentic expression and modeling self-regulation through mindfulness, movement, breath, and naming your experience out loud. The child is still observing how you manage the intensity of the emotions and sensations that are arising. You're still helping support the rewiring of children's neural networks as they move toward their dysregulated states with your help as the external regulator.

THE SIGNIFICANCE OF THE OBSERVER

For those of you who use a play therapy style that allows the child to choose whether you'll be an active participant in the play or watch the play, have you ever considered the possibility that being placed in the observer role isn't random? What if I told you that when a child chooses to put you in the observer role, that's also part of the setup?

Consider these scenarios: Toby witnessed domestic violence between his parents; Sheila was forced to watch her sibling be sexually violated; Max saw his mom killed in a car accident; Leila walked into her living room and found her mom passed out on the floor after drinking too much. How would these children help you understand what it felt like to be them? One of the ways is by making you an observer.

So if you use a style of play therapy that naturally puts you in the observer role, you aren't off the hook—the setup is still taking place. The child will still do whatever it takes to help you understand what it feels like to be him or her, and your nervous system will still be affected by the intensity.

HOW TO BE AN OBSERVER

One of the biggest considerations is that what you say has to make sense. For example, if the child is hurting the baby doll and the therapist is crying as if he or she is the baby, the child will probably wonder or say, "You're not hurting. Why are you crying? The baby's down there. You're fine." Kids will stop in the middle of the play because they're confused and momentarily disoriented by the incongruence. It's confusing to them because it doesn't make sense. And we know that when something doesn't make sense in the environment, the child's brain will pause and orient toward the confusion to try to figure it out. When this happens, children get pulled out of their experience and into their analytical thinking as they try to make sense of the incongruence. Our goal is to have the child spend as much time in self-reflection as possible, and making statements that make sense facilitates this. Here are three types of congruent reflections that are important to know:

Observational Statements

Observational statements describe what therapists are observing as they track the child's play. Examples include:

"The cars are crashing into each other."

"There's a monster in the house" (watching the child play with a monster in a dollhouse).

"Superman and Batman are fighting each other" (watching the child make the superheroes hit each other).

These types of statements also have a regulatory effect for you as the therapist because they help you oscillate between the intensity of your inner experience and the experience you're observing. Being able to use self-reflective statements and statements that describe what you're noticing the child do is great modeling for the child, because the child gets to witness the therapist using mindfulness to be aware of self and other (dual attention), a significant part of the attachment process. When you make observational statements, be sure to simply state the obvious, without interpretation. "Just the facts and only the facts," I tell my students.

Authentic Experience as the Observer

As the observer, it's important that you vocalize what it's like to be the observer. What does it feel like to have to watch whatever it is you're being asked to watch? Are you nervous? Do you feel helpless? Does your stomach hurt? Are you confused? Are you scared? If you're watching a fight, do you know why the fighting is happening? When the child sets you up as the observer, it's because he or she needs you to feel what it's like to observe and not be able to do anything about what's occurring. I find this to be especially common among children who have witnessed domestic violence. If therapists aren't willing to say what it feels like to observe the fighting, they're potentially missing a huge piece of the experience.

Let's consider the following session. Lonnie, who is 4 years old, placed a baby doll on the couch and told the therapist that the baby was drowning. The therapist immediately began to express the sense of fear and as she stood there watching the baby drown. "The baby! Help! No one is helping the baby! I'm scared! I want to save the baby!" She was also regulating through the intensity as she shook her arms, rocked back and forth, and put her hand on her chest to support her breathing. Lonnie had watched his younger brother drown when he was 2 years old and couldn't do anything to save him. He needed the therapist to understand, and so he set her up to observe a baby drowning. As they played through this event, Lonnie's own nervous system moved from a dorsal response toward mobilization as he observed his therapist attuning to him and modeling self-regulation. In the midst of the intensity, he began to modulate the energy in his own nervous system by taking deep breaths and moving alongside the therapist.

Voicing the Toy

The last type of reflection for observers is to voice what the toy is feeling. Again, it's very important for the therapist to make sense when doing this. We don't want the child to spend time trying to figure the therapist out. We want the therapist's reflections to help deepen children's play experience and understanding of themselves. One of the easiest ways to do this is to make statements like "If I were the (name the toy), I would be feeling . . ." or "If I were the (name the toy), I would be thinking . . ." With these types of statements, the therapist is staying congruent, and the child doesn't have to spend time trying to make sense of what the therapist has just said. In the example of the crying baby that I mentioned earlier in this chapter, the therapist could say, "If I were the baby, I would be hurting and crying," and then cry as if she were the baby. The therapist could also use the other types of reflections to help deepen the play while still being congruent.

Ask yourself these questions to help you reflect what you are observing:

- Does what I'm saying make sense?
- Am I being authentic?
- Am I being congruent with what I am experiencing and expressing?
- Am I stating just the facts, or am I adding in interpretation?

USING THE BOP BAG/PUNCHING BAG

Some play therapists believe that using bop bags/punching bags promotes aggression in children, while others believe it's an essential toy to the playroom, allowing children to express themselves fully and thus encouraging empowerment.

In an effort to bridge these opinions, let's explore how to use the bop bag in ways that avoid promoting aggression while encouraging children to understand their need to express aggression. Please note that the examples listed below are just examples. There are many possibilities that are effective for deepening children's awareness of themselves when they use a bop bag. Follow your intuition, and trust your experience. The key is to help support mindfulness and integration, not just use the bop bag for cathartic purposes. It's also important to note that the bop bag is a versatile toy and is not limited to one type of use in the playroom. Although most children will use the bop bag as a way to project their feelings of disempowerment or empowerment, other children will use it as a source of comfort, leaning and resting on it for support, or as a sensory toy, bouncing and rolling on it to help regulate their nervous systems (to give just two examples of other ways a bop bag can be used).

Here are a few key guidelines to follow when a child chooses to use the bop bag:

- Don't assume you know who or what the child wants the bop bag to represent. It's not important for you to know.
- Unless you know the intended gender of the bop bag, it's best to refer to the bop bag as "it."
- Make reflections that address the underlying feelings the child is attempting to project onto the bop bag.
- As much as possible, avoid reflections that encourage aggression. Examples of reflections that encourage aggression are "Get him," "You are so strong," "Show him how mad you are," "Hit him again."
- Match the intensity of the play. The child will keep turning the play up until the therapist embodies or names the intensity. The most important principle to be aware of when children work with the bop bag in an aggressive way is that your ability to stay present and connected to yourself and to the children during the high level of intensity is the most healing aspect of the experience. If the children become highly dysregulated and their aggression escalates, it's your ability to stay regulated and emotionally and energetically

present that will ground the children. You can always acknowledge and redirect if needed.
- Remember, the goal is integration, not catharsis.

Imagine a child picks up the bop bag and starts throwing it around the room, turning it upside down, and making it spin quickly, and you're having to get out of the way to protect yourself. Here are some examples of effective responses that you could use:

- Voice the bop bag: "If I were it/him/her, I'd be thinking, 'I'm spinning out of control. My world is upside down.'"
- Voice what it's like to be the observer: "I am scared and nervous watching this fighting."
- Voice your observation of the bop bag: "Its world is turned upside down, and it has no control."
- Voice your observation of the child's interaction with the bop bag: "You want it/him/her to know what it feels like to have everything upside down and to have no control."

If children choose to use the bop bag for support or as a way to regulate, provide reflections that enhance their awareness of what they're doing.

Bobby is 10 and running around the playroom in an anxious and frantic way, going from toy to toy. He finds the bop bag and lies on top of it, struggling to gain his balance. Here are some examples of effective responses:

- Voice your observation of the bop bag: "It keeps moving. It's hard for it/him/her to keep steady and support you."
- Voice your observation of the child's interaction with the bop bag: "You're trying so hard to make it stop moving so that you can relax on top. It's so hard to find a way to relax when things just keeps moving."

The general guidelines for working with a child and a bop bag are essentially the same no matter what toy the child is choosing to play with.

In the next two chapters, I will share with you more tips and ideas for facilitating aggression and integrating the intensity in both hyper-aroused and hypo-aroused play.

CHAPTER 11 KEY POINTS

- Even when you are an observer, your nervous system will still be affected by the intensity in the play, and children will still attempt to show you how they feel through the setup.
- As the observer, it is important to have an authentic and congruent response based on what it feels like to be the observer of the child's play.

- When observing play, make observational statements that are just the facts, without interpretation.
- It is still important to regulate as an observer, as children still need to borrow your regulatory capacity to help them integrate their challenging internal thoughts, feelings, and sensations.
- The bop bag is a versatile toy and is not limited to one type of use in the playroom. It is important that it is used for integration, not catharsis.

Hyper-Aroused Play

SCOTT, AGE 7, PUT THE BLOCKS AWAY AND SAT beside me on the floor, and I felt a strange anxiety enter my body. I noticed that my breathing was changing. I noticed that the energy in the room had changed, almost as if the room were holding its breath. Just as I registered these changes, Scott grabbed a snake puppet and threw it toward me. Imagining for a second that it was a real snake coming toward me, I shrieked, as I had been given no protection. And then I took a deep breath, allowing the tension to release from my body. Next a spider came at me, and then a dragon, and then a shark. I authentically said things like, "I don't understand why this is happening. I'm scared. I have no protection. I don't know if I am going to get hurt." Scott was giving me a window into his world.

The play was filled with hyper-arousal. In order to help him integrate the intensity, I did everything that I have taught you how to do in this book. I allowed the experience to feel real while holding the knowledge that it wasn't real. I stayed present and used mindfulness to expand my window of tolerance to hold the intensity. I used movement and breath and named my experience to regulate the energy in my nervous system and in his play. This also helped him stay connected to himself and not emotionally flood.

Scott had been a witness to domestic violence, and through his play, he set me up to understand the hypervigilance and fear that he experienced. In his play, he would scare me with the animals, but the animals never actually hurt me. He helped me understand what it felt like to be him, always wondering if he would get hurt and not being able to predict when the violence would start.

Before we discuss more ways to work with hyper-arousal in the playroom, I want you to take a moment and refer back to the nervous system chart in Chapter 3 to refresh yourself with the symptoms of hyper-arousal. I also want to remind you that if we don't regulate during intense play, we risk increasing the intensity in the play because the child is attempting to get us to have an authentic response, and we also risk experiencing vicarious trauma and compassion fatigue.

MORE ON REGULATING THROUGH HYPER-AROUSAL

Let's explore using breath and naming experience a bit more to help you when hyper-aroused intensity enters the play.

Breathe!

When hyper-arousal enters the playroom, you will probably notice a tightening in your body, along with shallow breathing or holding your breath. These are natural responses when we're scared or we feel intensity in our bodies. However, when our breathing becomes shallow and we hold our breath, it actually intensifies the experience, contributes to hyperventilation and keeps the hyper-aroused energy going.

As you begin to experience the hyper-aroused energy in the room, and you notice your breathing becoming faster and shallower, it's important to elongate your exhale to ground and release the energy. Sometimes the play is happening so quickly, like in a sword fight, that it's hard to take a deep breath. In these moments, remind yourself to take a deep breath between the hits and swings.

Use your breath to help ground you in the intensity and keep your nervous system regulated. The benefit to the children is that they will hear your breathing which reminds them to breathe.

Be Vocal!

If you have an animal biting you or you're watching a doll being hit or thrown onto the floor, this is not the time to be quiet (unless you've been set up to have no voice or are silenced in some way in the play). This is the time to share your experience out loud by describing what it's like for you to observe the aggression. This is the time to be real! In doing so, you may find yourself screaming or saying things like "I'm scared," "I don't know how to protect myself," "Ouch!" "I don't even understand why I'm fighting," or maybe even "Why is this happening to me? I'm worried about the baby." There isn't a "right" thing to say in the midst of the intensity. Whatever is true for you in the moment is what's important to vocalize.

Remember that naming your experience out loud supports integration, as it is able to calm both your and the child's amygdalae (Siegel & Bryson, 2011).

And remember that making observational statements about what the child is literally doing is just as important as sharing our own experience out loud in the play. This will help both you and the child orient to what is happening in the play, as well as keep the prefrontal cortex engaged.

FEEL IT AND LET IT GO

I want you to imagine that you're a martial artist and that an opponent is coming at you. What do you do? Do you stop the opponent by saying, "No, you can't do that"? Do you walk away? No, you move toward the opponent mindfully. When your opponent strikes, you don't move away from the strike. Instead, you meet it. You allow yourself to be present with the intensity, and then you let it go. And then the next strike comes. You again meet it, you're present with, and you let it go.

We can see the same process in yoga when we face a challenge. Maybe you hit a place of tightness in your body or are about to lose your balance. What do you do? You lean in toward the challenge mindfully, being present with the sensations, and then, using your breath, you release, letting go into the pose. The point is, as the child's intensity comes toward us, we practice being present with ourselves and with the energy itself. We practice allowing ourselves to feel the setup and the intensity. We remember the mantra "one foot in and one foot out." We give ourselves permission to have an authentic reaction to whatever is occurring, and then we let it all go. We can repeat this with each wave of intensity that comes toward us.

The session I had with 4-year-old Henry illustrates this practice. I was smashed between my chair and my couch, curled up to protect myself while Henry hissed at me and threw burning poison on me. In the context of the play, I was oscillating between responding as if burning poison was literally being thrown on me and barely being able to get the words out as the poison covered my body. "My body is hurting," "Ouch," "It's on fire!" "Make it stop!" "I can't breathe," "I'm scared," "I don't trust," "It isn't safe"—those were some of the things I said. He came at me again, hissing in my face in a primal, animalistic way, and my body tightened. Allowing myself to stay present in the experience but not be consumed by it, I silently reminded myself that I was in a play therapy session. I breathed. I breathed a lot. I focused on the exhale of my breath to allow for some release to occur as I was being set up to understand the fear that Henry has experienced in his trauma. I wiggled my toes, because they were the only parts of my body I could move, as I was crammed in a small space. I felt the intensity in my body and then let it go. I came back to myself. And then Henry came at me again, hissing and this time pressing a pillow against me, creating more pressure. He wanted me to have an experience of what it would feel like to be enveloped in overwhelm, pain, and terror and unable to do anything to make it stop. As I felt his world, I allowed myself to feel it, name it, move it, and let it go.

LET'S SWORD FIGHT!

Whether it was playing cowboys and Indians or cops and robbers or having pillow fights as children, most of us have experienced the energy of a play fight. And typically we were laughing, fighting back equally hard, being competitive and silly and playful. Sword fights are common in play therapy sessions, but they're often very different from standard childhood fights, as they aren't typically accompanied by fun and playfulness.

Here are some tips for facilitating sword fights in the playroom to make them therapeutic. Keep in mind that these are general guidelines and not rules. If children need something different to occur, they'll let you know. Most important, trust your intuition.

Don't Win—Lose Your Power Slowly

Just like in other forms of play, in sword fights children are attempting to set you up to feel how they feel, which typically is powerless. They're coming in feeling disempowered and struggling to integrate their perception of a challenge that they're experiencing or have experienced.

It's important to lose your power. Let yourself feel what it's like to feel helpless because you don't have enough power, you're not strong enough, and you can't protect yourself well.

A great way to help you lose your power is to get yourself backed into a corner or a couch so that you can slowly fall to the floor or onto the couch, becoming smaller and smaller.

Don't Be Too Good

Children need a worthy opponent, but if you're too good, the fight becomes more about defeating you as the therapist, not to mention that the child has to work really hard. It's also important to get down to their height level as best you can and sword fight from there.

I saw a great example of a therapist being too good a sword fighter during one of our Synergetic Play Therapy intensive trainings. The therapist was a tall woman, and her client was a 5-year-old boy half her size. As he began the sword fight, she remained standing tall and swung her sword high above his head. The result was that the child couldn't take her power away easily. He was jumping and swinging up high to try to get her sword. He tried everything he could think of to get her to go down, which is where he needed her to be in order for her to feel helpless and powerless. He tried to stab her, he fought with two swords, he even pulled up a chair to stand on, but nothing worked. In the end, he took his sword and swiped her legs to "cut them off," and she finally got the message and went down.

Do I Fight Back?

Whether you fight back depends on a number of factors. I've been in sword fights where the sword was coming at me so strong and fast that I couldn't fight back even if I wanted to! Other times, the child will go slowly and then speed it up, lunging at you and teasing you. You may get your arms cut off immediately and have no protection. There are so many variations, but what matters most is the context and the energy that's arising as a result of how the sword fight is playing out.

If you're able to fight back, then of course fight back if that's what seems authentic, but follow these two important guidelines:

- Sometimes the child will say, "Attack me!" or "Cut off my leg!" or something like that. If the child tells you to attack him with a sword, do it very carefully and gently. Have the child dictate exactly what you're supposed to do.

- At any point if the sword fight feels like too much, or what is being asked of you doesn't feel OK to you, set a boundary by acknowledging and redirecting the play.

I've observed that therapists who have a high need for control or who don't like the feeling of losing or being powerless will sometimes get in a little jab. Maybe it's a quick little hit to the child's leg when there's a lull in the energy or a quick little stab when they aren't looking. Sometimes it's hard to lose our power, and we want a moment of feeling powerful. If this arises in the playroom, acknowledge your need to yourself, breathe, and then give yourself permission to feel the uncomfortable feelings you're trying to avoid.

SCRIPTING THE PLAY

When children ask you to hit them with your sword (or shoot them or handcuff them or anything else that seems aggressive), it's extremely important that the child is able to script what follows. This is typically a time in the therapy process when the children need you to become the challenge so that they can empower themselves. When this happens, pause and ask the child to tell you exactly how to do it.

For example, when Jennifer, age 8, and I were sword fighting, she had two swords and a shield, and I had nothing. I was being set up to feel completely powerless with absolutely no way to protect myself. All of a sudden, she handed me her swords and shield.

"Now you get me," she said.

I paused for a moment and became present. "Do you want me to do it exactly how you did it to me, or in another way?" I asked.

"Just like I did to you," she said.

As I approached her to begin the sword fight, I remained mindful of my breathing and was careful not to do anything that I hadn't seen her do before. Just as I was about to swing at her legs, she threw a magic potion on me that turned me into a statue, reclaiming her power.

If children ask you to do something that you feel completely uncomfortable doing, or you are questioning whether the way they want you to do something might actually reinforce a trauma experience, acknowledge and redirect. This also goes for any play, whether children are asking you to do something to them or not. Whatever you do, though, keep the energy moving.

CHAPTER 11 KEY POINTS

- Regulate, regulate, regulate!
- When intensity and hyper-arousal occur, it is important to tune in to your breath, elongating your exhalation if you notice your breathing becoming shallow.
- As you begin to feel the intensity from hyper-aroused play, feel it, name it, move it, and let it go.
- Remind yourself that it is important to feel the setup in the play but not get absorbed in the play, believing you are actually getting hurt.
- Sword-fighting guide: Lose your power slowly, don't be too good, and script the play if at any point children ask you to become the challenger and do something to them.

Hypo-Aroused Play

I WALK INTO THE WAITING ROOM TO GREET 5-YEAR-old Jenny, who is sitting next to her mom. I lean down to say hello, and Jenny bolts out of her chair and runs down the hallway. I'm so stunned that there isn't time to register my feelings. I turn and run after her. As I try to catch up, I see her run into my playroom. Just as I cross the threshold of the playroom door, Jenny pulls out a toy gun and shoots me. I'm dead and remain that way for the rest of the session. All I could think was, "I didn't even get to say hi."

IS DEATH IN THE PLAYROOM REALLY NECESSARY?

Jenny was adopted at birth. In many ways, she had the picture-perfect adoption story. Her birth mother was a high-functioning 16-year-old from a good home who decided that she wasn't ready to be a mother. After she made the decision to place Jenny up for adoption, she handpicked the adoptive parents. Jenny's adoptive parents were involved during the entire pregnancy and were also in the room at the time of the delivery. When Jenny emerged into the world, she was placed into her adoptive mother's arms.

She had to kill me because I had to know what it felt like to want to say hello and connect and to then feel completely abandoned, rejected, and not wanted. I needed to understand the level of abandonment and shock that she experienced.

Children who are experiencing a degree of emotional numbing, dissociation, emotional constriction, and depression often present in a hypo-aroused state. Remember that when we perceive a challenge that's so big that we think we can't do anything about it, or it's gone on too long or is too intense, the nervous system naturally goes into a dorsal-activated hypo-aroused state for the sake of self-preservation. For children who are having this experience, death play may be a very important part of the therapy. Death can also be used as part of the setup to let the therapist know what it feels like to be helpless, unimportant, and deeply rejected, and even want to just disappear. Death play may also be literal for some children who have witnessed a death or experienced the loss of a loved one.

Therapists may have fears about whether playing with death promotes death. Similar to aggression, there can be a fear that if they play dead or allow death to occur, they're promoting scary behavior outside the playroom. It's important to remember that just like in aggressive play, the thera-pist's ability to stay present, regulate, and model mindfulness in the midst of the intensity during this type of play helps promote integration. When therapists are checking out, not naming the intensity of the emotions that are arising in the play, and not present with what's occurring in their bodies and in the relationship with the child, the therapists take the risk that the child will need to take the play outside the room to continue the attempts at integration.

If the idea of exploring death in the playroom is a chal-lenging thought for you, keep in mind that kids have been playing dead throughout recorded history, in every culture. It's normal for children to be curious about the death pro-cess. Children are surrounded by death and endings every day. The playroom is the perfect place to explore the emo-tions and sensations that arise as children process this important part of the life experience.

FALLING TO YOUR DEATH

Over the years, through much trial and error—some com-ical and some painful—I've learned that there is indeed a helpful way to fall when you die. It's important to die in a way that protects you from being hurt and allows you to maintain knowledge of what's happening in the room with the child. It's also important to stay dead until you are told you're alive again or until the session is over.

In one session, I was told that I was a robber and had

to try to rob the bank. As I sneaked toward the cash register, Margaret called out for me to turn toward her and put my hands in the air. I put my hands in the air, and as I turned around, she shot me. I stumbled back, and she shot me again. My body responded as if I were really being shot. Recognizing that I was probably dead at this point, I fell. Unfortunately, I didn't plan my fall, and as I fell backward, my back went right into the corner of the sand tray. Ouch. I landed on my back, completely exposed, with my arms out wide. Next thing I knew, she was stabbing a sword into my gut. Ouch again.

Here are some suggestions for keeping yourself safe when you need to die in the playroom.

- Fall onto something soft. If you're shot, stabbed, or pretend punched, you can always stumble back into or onto something comfy like a couch or a chair.
- When you fall, make sure you fall in a way that protects your head and stomach. Curl up if possible. If you fall onto your back with your stomach and heart exposed, you have a high probability of being shot or stabbed there. Trust me!
- Don't fully close your eyes. If you do, you'll feel very vulnerable, which can induce feelings of hypervigilance. You also won't be able to track the child. It's OK to have your eyes open and stare into the distance. With your eyes open, you can use your peripheral vision to see what's happening.

- Make sure that however you fall, you fall facing the center of the room so that your back isn't turned away from what the child is doing.
- If you have to fall to the floor, fall into the fetal position. Land in a position where you're resting your head on one extended arm for support while placing the other over the top of your head. In doing so, you'll create a gap between your arms that you can peek through.

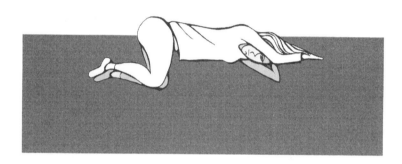

DEAD PEOPLE DON'T TALK

When therapists die, it's important that they don't talk. I've seen therapists repeatedly attempt to talk while they're dead, and each time they were killed again. Talking while dead actually prolongs the process. I've also noticed that the desire to talk while dead typically comes from therapists' desire to not have to feel everything they are feeling while

dead. Many times it's also a way for therapists to reestab-
lish a sense of being in control, because—let's be honest—
playing dead is a very helpless and out-of-control experience.

There are three exceptions to the rule against talking
while dead:

- If the child is young and a lot of time goes by, it's
  important to remind them that they can make you
  come alive again. You can sit up quickly and whisper,
  "You're in charge and can make me be alive whenever
  you want," and then lie back down.
- Just because you're dead doesn't mean you don't have
  to be aware of time. It's still important to tell the child
  they have 10 minutes left or 5 minutes or 1 minute.
- Being dead doesn't mean you can no longer set
  boundaries when you need to. If you're dead and the
  child is continuing to stab you or tries to hurt you,
  it's important that you give yourself permission to set
  a boundary.

REGULATING THROUGH HYPO-AROUSAL AND DEATH

Playing dead can be just as intense as aggressive play, if
not more so. Hypo-arousal regulation can be challenging,
because there isn't a lot of energy to work with, but it's essential to continue to use mindfulness, breath, movement, and
naming your experience out loud (when you're allowed to

talk) as part of the process. If you don't, you will experience high levels of numbing and potentially check out and disso- ciate. You're still registering the intensity on some level, and without regulation you'll probably feel the effects of the play sometime after the session.

Probably the most challenging part of facilitating hypo- aroused energy in death play is that when you're dead, you're not able to talk and you have to be still. For these reasons, regulation has to become an internal process. Even though you can't name your experience out loud or move outwardly, you can use mindfulness, breath, and internal movements to help facilitate the dysregulation in your nervous system and remain present. Even though you're dead, you still have a body! While you're lying there, remind yourself that you are in the play as you feel the setup, and that it's still import- ant to practice regulation through the intense sensations you might be experiencing. Here are some tips for regulating your body so that you can stay present and attuned to the child.

Breathe, Breathe, Breathe

Even in hypo-aroused play, one of the best ways to regulate yourself and keep yourself present is through your breath.

While you're dead, practice regulated breathing. This is especially helpful when you have to be dead for an extended period of time. You regulate your breathing by making your inhalation and your exhalation the same length of time. Sometimes it's even helpful to silently count during the breaths. As you breathe in, slowly count one-two-three-four, and as you breathe out, slowly count one-two-three-four. Continue to repeat the cycle. It doesn't matter what number you count to as long as it feels comfortable to you.

Reflection

Lie on the floor as if you're dead and practice regulated breathing for 1 minute.

Do Body Scans

Another strategy for keeping yourself present is a body scan. Using mindfulness, place your attention on your feet, pausing to notice them. You may find that they feel quite active inside, or you may notice that you can't feel them. Just notice. Then turn your attention to other parts of your body, each time pausing and noticing how they feel.

As you notice parts of your body, you may want to move them. If this is the case, find ways of moving that aren't visible to the child. Wiggling your toes in your shoes, tightening and releasing your muscles, and pressing your body into the floor or couch are some ways you can bring subtle movement into death play. For optimal regulation, you might even consider doing movements that are bilaterally oriented (*bilateral* means "affecting both sides"). For example, alternately tighten the muscles in your left leg and your right leg. This activates both the right and left hemispheres of your brain, promoting integration.

YOU STILL HAVE FEELINGS!

Even though you're dead, you're still being set up to feel the children's perception of themselves and the challenging experiences they've gone through. As you're lying there, ask yourself, "How am I feeling right now? Do I feel lonely? Do I feel sad? Do I feel helpless? Did I never even have a chance for survival? Do I feel unimportant? Do I feel relief because I don't want to deal with the intensity of hyper-arousal or aggression anymore?" (The last question reflects a common feeling when death occurs after a period of high-intensity aggressive play.)

As you feel the setup, be aware of the dysregulation in your body while not getting swept up in it. Hold a larger view of what is happening in the playroom so that you can continue to attune to yourself and to the child.

Even though you can't say these things out loud, you're acknowledging to yourself how you're feeling, and you'll still experience the regulatory benefit. As you silently acknowledge your feelings, you allow yourself to move toward these feelings, staying connected to yourself in the midst of the intensity of the hypo-aroused response but not getting lost in it.

YOU STILL HAVE A MIND!

You'll notice that while lying there dead, your mind will start to wander. You may start to plan your grocery-shopping list or think about anything that gets your mind's attention and keeps you from feeling what's happening in the room. This is a natural experience, and it will happen. You may also feel sleepy or want to zone out. When this occurs, simply notice it and come back to yourself by turning your attention to your body and your breath. If you've managed to die with your eyes open or someplace where you can peek, become aware of what's happening in the room. Become aware of the child.

THE CHILD CAN FEEL YOU

You might be wondering why it's so important to go to such great lengths to manage the hypo-aroused state you're in. The answer is because the child can feel you. You are still the external regulator.

After a short but intense sword fight, Lily stabbed me in the heart and announced my death. Luckily, I had been able to fall into a fetal position facing the play, so I could peek out under my arm to track where she was in the room. I used mindfulness and my breath to be with my experience and stay connected to myself as I felt her setup. As I did this, I noticed that I was also able to stay connected to Lily. For the next 25 minutes, Lily wandered around the room seeming a bit lost, but she eventually made her way to the sand tray and quietly felt the sand and put it into containers. She never looked in my direction or came over to me. After 10 more minutes passed, I noticed that it was getting harder for me to remain present with myself. Then my mind decided to completely wander as I began to think about my day and what I was going to do that evening. I disconnected from myself and let go of the energetic container I was holding for Lily. I was no longer present. The moment this happened, Lily stood up from the sand tray and walked straight over to me and kicked me. She'd felt me leave her.

STAYING PRESENT WHILE DEAD

Let me be really honest: It's hard to stay present during hypo-aroused energy as the activation of the dorsal vagal nerve creates the experience of wanting to collapse and check out. The consensus from my students and my own personal experience is that navigating the waters of hypo-arousal is much harder than navigating hyper-arousal. It takes work and dedication to be with yourself when you're being ignored, dismissed, abandoned, and left to die in the play. For most play therapists, this experience brings up all kinds of uncomfortable emotions.

You might be wondering, "If you can't talk and can't move, how are you teaching regulation to a child by lying there?" Even though it may seem as if nothing is happening, much is occurring. When you're lying there mindfully regulating, you're affecting the energy in the room. You're still holding the container that allows children to move toward their uncomfortable feelings and sensations rather than avoiding them. In the silence, the children have the opportunity to feel their feelings that are connected to the play. Think of it like an attuned mother who is quietly regulating next to her sad or withdrawn child. The mother continues to act as the external regulator even when the child is hypo-aroused.

One of the strategies I use for helping me stay present during this kind of play is visualization. As I feel myself getting smaller and wanting to disappear or disengage, I imagine myself energetically getting as big as the room. I imagine this until energetically I feel bigger than the room and feel myself holding everything in it, including the child.

Reflection

Lie on the floor in the fetal position. You can practice the "death position" if you'd like. Now imagine yourself energetically expanding like a balloon, reaching out to the walls and up to the ceiling, filling every space possible in the room. Feel yourself getting bigger. Feel your presence in the room expand.

REPEATED DEATH

Sometimes a child will kill you multiple times in a session. You die and then you're told to come alive again, only to be faced with another death. This type of play can be exhausting and requires a high level of regulation, as your own nervous system will be flip-flopping between intense states of hyper-arousal and hypo-arousal. Remember that one of the stages of activation of the nervous system is called *dual autonomic activation*. This happens when both the sympathetic branch and the dorsal vagal nerve are attempting to take over at the same time. This is what it feels like. Part of you wants to fight, and part of you wants to collapse. Over time, the setup in this play can create feelings of just wanting to die and to stay dead. When this happens, the play is symbolically representing the activation of the dorsal branch wanting to check out and numb out for an extended period of time. It can also create feelings of helplessness and hopelessness, as therapists know that when they're alive in the play, their death is imminent. Over time, it can also create feelings of anger as therapists reach the "enough is enough" point but are unable to do anything about it. Remember, your authenticity and ability to model regulation through this is key.

DESCRIBING HYPO-AROUSAL

I'm sitting in front of 9-year-old Bobby as he lines up the army men on the floor. The energy in the room is very still. Everything seems to be happening in slow motion. My brain begins to tell me that a fight is going to happen, but I can't feel the anxiety. In fact, I can't feel much of anything. As I watch him set up the army men, I start to feel a little sleepy. When he's finished with the setup, Bobby picks up a soldier and in slow motion moves it to shoot another soldier. He makes a quiet gunshot sound. The sound drifts off, fading away. He picks up a different soldier and again slowly and quietly attacks another soldier. The war has begun, and although I can see it, I can't feel it.

As we're set up to watch play that involves death, we might also be set up to feel hypo-aroused. When this happens, we can get sleepy; feel numb, spacey, and bored; and have a hard time registering feelings in our bodies. This is also true when we've been in intense play for a period of time and our nervous systems just want to shut down, as in the case with repeated death. It registers in the brain as too much, and a dorsal-collapse response sets in.

You've already learned how to regulate through these intense states, but finding the words when you can't tell what you're experiencing can be challenging. Describing your experience of feeling hypo-aroused often involves describing the absence of sensations and emotions. For example, in Bobby's play, I said things like, "As I am watching you set up the army men, I can't feel anything in my body. My brain is telling me to be scared because there is a fight happening in front of me, but I just can't feel it." The reason this is significant is that the experience of observing something challenging and not being able to feel it can be very much a part of a trauma response. The body will do whatever it needs to do to manage the intensity it's experiencing. For many children who have experienced or observed trauma, it will be important for them to explore these states of the nervous system as they work toward repatterning the experiences. Allowing yourself to feel it helps you be able to regulate through it so that you can help the child do the same.

And don't forget to keep making lots of observational statements about the child's play!

NEGATIVE SELF-TALK

I have one final note on hypo-aroused play. Therapists who have had sessions filled with hypo-arousal often ask me questions like "What am I doing wrong? What am I missing?" They aren't missing anything. In fact, those thoughts are exactly what they're set up to ask. Negative self-talk is often the corresponding brain chatter associated with hypo-arousal. It's also part of the setup. When we're having a hypo-aroused response, it's easy to question ourselves, think we're not understanding something, and believe there's something wrong with us. We forget that this is all part of the setup and is most likely what the child is experiencing inside.

CHAPTER 13 KEY POINTS

- Death can be a symbolic representation of the hypo-aroused state of the nervous system.
- Death can be part of the setup to let us know what it feels like to be helpless, unimportant, and deeply rejected.
- During hypo-aroused play, it is important to feel, regulate, and attune, because children can still feel you and still need your presence as they work toward integrating their dysregulation.
- Mindfulness practices, body scans, and using your

breath while "dead" are effective ways to regulate when you aren't able to move or talk.

- Sometimes describing the experience of hypo-arousal requires describing the absence of sensation and emotion, as the dorsal collapse creates a numbing experience in the body.

Supporting Parents During Aggressive Play

"Mom, will you come into the room and play with us today?" asks 6-year-old Ellen. Mom looks up at the therapist to see whether or not it would be OK to come along. The therapist nods, indicating that it is OK for her to join.

The three of them enter the playroom, and Ellen immediately starts her play. She pulls out a baby horse and a tiger figurine. Right away, the tiger starts to attack the baby horse, biting it and violently hurting it. The mom is in shock and doesn't know what to do or say but is clearly overwhelmed watching her daughter play this way. She quickly looks at her daughter and says, "Ellen, be nice to the horse. It isn't OK to play like that." Ellen looks at her mom and then looks at the therapist, waiting to see how the therapist will respond.

Aggression is not only challenging for therapists, it is also challenging for parents. Whether the parent is in the room observing the play, is asked to be a part of the play itself, or is struggling with the child's aggression at home, parents need just as much support as their children do.

There are many theories about working with parents. Some therapists advocate for the parents to always be in the playroom. Some therapists prefer to not have the parents in the room at all and to work with the parents only separately from the child. Others do a combination.

It doesn't matter what theory you work from as long as working with the parents is part of your practice. This chapter will address how to work with parents when they end up in your playroom and aggressive play begins.

Imagine these scenarios. A child you are working with grabs a toy gun, sword, or a pair of handcuffs and tries to shoot, stab, or handcuff his mom. Maybe he attempts to do this to you while his mother watches. Maybe the child attempts to dump all of the bins of toys on the floor or throw them across the room. What do you do? How do you make this therapeutic? And more importantly, how do you begin to work with the mother, whose nervous system has most likely become dysregulated?

The most important thing to understand is that the moment you have a parent join your play therapy sessions, you are now responsible for the regulation of three nervous systems—yours, the child's, and the parent's.

Olivia, age 3, grabbed her mom's arm in the waiting room, motioning for her to come into the playroom. This was only the third session, and she had not wanted her mom in the room for the first two. The therapist welcomed Olivia's desire, and the three of them went in together.

Once they entered the room, Mom took a seat on a stool to watch. Olivia and the therapist proceeded to sit on the floor next to Mom, and Olivia began her play. She pulled out the toy soldiers and started to reenact a war. Feelings of anxiety and hypervigilance immediately began to fill the room, as it wasn't clear whether or not many of the soldiers were safe. The therapist began to track Olivia's play, making observational statements about what she was doing. As the therapist tracked the play, she wasn't regulating, modulating the energy, or naming the scary emotions in the room, and the intensity began to build. Olivia's play became more and more violent, but not to the point where a boundary was needed. It was simply intense. As the intensity increased, the therapist continued to play with her, making observational statements, and her mom continued to watch.

As the play became more aggressive, the mother visibly became uncomfortable, and her body began to tighten. Signs of the dorsal parasympathetic response began to emerge, as it was clear that the intensity was starting to feel "too much." The mother was beginning to emotionally flood. The therapist, sitting on the floor and focused on the child, had no idea that this was happening.

This was a play session I observed during a supervision session. As I watched the recorded video, I was able to see the play unfolding, and I was able to see how everyone's nervous systems were attempting to manage the intensity. I was also aware that this child had witnessed domestic violence between her mom and dad. I knew that her dad had been removed from the home after he physically assaulted the mother. As the mother sat there observing the play, what she was really observing was the violence that she herself had experienced. Her daughter was reenacting the aggression right in front of her eyes, and as a result, she was reliving the experience of her own trauma, without any support to integrate what was happening for her.

As I've already shared, when children don't feel the presence, authenticity, and regulatory capacity of the therapist, they will turn the play up a notch until the therapist has no choice but to show up. The same is true with parents. Children need to feel their parents, and when they don't, they also turn it up a notch until they do. This speaks to the importance of working with the parent in the session to become the external regulator. Teaching parents to understand what children are saying through their play is only part of what needs to happen. The other part is to teach parents how to modulate and regulate the energy in their own bodies, so that they can model to their children how to do the same.

What happened next in the session was a big learning experience for the therapist.

The mother started to shut down even further as the intensity increased, and she eventually dissociated. The moment this happened, the child reached behind her and grabbed a toy sword, and with the therapist unable to stop it, she swung it at her mother, hitting her across the face. The trauma was reenacted.

Obviously, this affected everyone in the session, and it took some repair to help establish a neuroception of safety again, but it was established, and both the child and her mother were able to have a positive and integrative play therapy experience.

This is such an important story to share, as it highlights the purpose of this chapter so beautifully. I am so grateful for the courage it took for this therapist to share this video with me, so that she could begin to learn how to work with parents in the playroom in new ways that supported a deeper level of integration without having anyone's nervous systems start to flood and shut down.

Whenever a supervisee brings to me a session with the parent in the room, one of the first questions I ask is, "Where was the parent?" Often, when parents are in session, they are sitting in the corner watching or sitting up in a chair away from the play that is happening between the therapist and the child. Often they are just observing.

When a parent is in the room, you have two clients, and it is your task to teach them how to play and interact together. This means that the parent needs to be on the floor right next to you.

Just as therapists often feel overwhelmed and scared by aggression, parents do, too. Their own beliefs about whether or not aggression is OK, their past experiences with aggression, and their own ability to stay connected to themselves in the midst of intensity will influence their window of tol-erance in the playroom. What this literally translates into is whether or not parents will be able to stay present when aggression emerges in the playroom or whether they will try to shut it down.

For these reasons, it is so important that the therapist teach parents how to become another external regulator in the room, so that they can support the child when aggres-sion arises in the playroom. If we don't teach parents how to do this, they miss out on learning the skills they need to support their child when the aggression shows up outside of the playroom. We also increase the probability that parents will leave the session feeling overwhelmed and traumatized and possibly not want to come back again.

IT IS TIME TO COACH!

As we have already explored, children need to borrow the regulatory capacity of an adult as they learn how to manage the energy inside themselves. This means not only that we need to learn how to strengthen our own regulatory capacity and expand our window of tolerance, but that we need to teach parents how to do the same.

In Synergetic Play Therapy, when a parent enters the playroom, the therapist becomes a coach. In an ideal sce-nario, the therapist would have known that the parent was going to be a part of the session and would have scheduled a time to meet prior to the session for a training session. This training session would be a time for therapists to teach the parents what to expect in the playroom, practice some of the skills that they would want parents to use, and create a deeper sense of connection with parents so that the therapists can support the parents in the room when needed. As a reminder, the unknown is a threat to the brain, so let's prepare the parents we work with by helping them understand what to expect and setting them up for success.

REGULATING THE PARENT IN THE PLAYROOM

Let's go back to the session with Olivia, when her mom came in and sat on the stool, watching. How could this session have been handled differently to prevent the flooding that her mother experienced and to support Olivia's integration of the thoughts, feelings, and sensations that were arising in her as her play became more aggressive? Let's explore some options.

- The therapist could have advocated for the mom not to join the session if the therapist felt that it wasn't appropriate without a training session, given the nature of what Olivia was working on.
- The therapist could have taken a more directive approach to create more containment in the play, while determining the mother's readiness and window of tolerance for a nondirective approach.
- If a nondirective approach was chosen, the therapist

could have asked the mother to sit on the floor next to her. (If there were physical reasons why the mother could not have done this, the stool could have been moved right next to the therapist, or the therapist might have also sat on a stool next to the mother.)

- Once in the play, the therapist could have begun to modulate the intensity using all of the skills that have been explored in this book, in addition to using observational statements to track the play. Naming her internal experience out loud to stay present with the sensations and soothe the amygdala, elongating the breath to ground the energy, and using movement to integrate the intensity are all options. As the therapist did this, she would also encourage the mother to do the same.

- As the therapist noticed the mother's body begin to tighten, she could have either paused the play to allow the mother to regulate or could have encouraged the mother to regulate as the intensity was increasing. Yes, it is absolutely OK to pause the play when a parent is in the room!

- What matters most is that the therapist becomes the regulator for all of the nervous systems in the room, whether a directive or nondirective approach is taken.

One of the most brilliant parts about working with parents like this in the playroom is that children get to observe the parents taking care of themselves. You can liken this to a baby's experience when it feels its parent begin to ground and get present in the midst of the intensity of the baby's screams and dysregulation. The act of doing this allows the ventral vagus nerve to activate, bringing the feeling of safety into the moment (Bullard, 2015). This is a very important step in the co-regulation between parent and child. As parents begin to regulate, children begin to borrow their regulatory capacity.

The therapist regulates the parent so that the parent can regulate the child.

SETTING BOUNDARIES

Before we begin to discuss setting boundaries in the playroom when a parent is in the session, there is a larger boundary that needs to be explored first. This boundary is the decision of whether or not it is useful for the parent to be in the session in the first place, especially if you know that aggression might be part of the play.

Think of the decision to have the parents in the room as part of your treatment plan. If the parents need to be in there in order to accomplish the goal, then have them in there. If you don't know why they are in there, then they probably don't need to be in there. If the parents are going to be in the session, you need to know why they are in there.

There are so many considerations that need to be thought through when deciding whether or not to have a parent in the room.

- Do I know the parent's trauma history?
- Does the parent want to be in the session? (Sometimes a resistant parent in the room can create a barrier, so the therapist needs to be willing to work with the resistance.)
- How wide is the parent's window of tolerance for what the child is trying to integrate?
- How developed is the parent's regulatory capacity?
- How emotionally available is the parent?

These are all questions that the therapist will have to consider when deciding the approach to use when the parent enters the room, especially if you suspect that aggressive play will be part of the child's process. If you answer "No" or "Not very well" to these questions, it doesn't mean that it isn't useful to have parents in the room. It does mean that you will need to work with parents even more to help prepare them for the sessions or choose a more directive approach to help create more containment.

Even if you decide not to have the parent in the session, it is still extremely important that you work with the parent separately. I understand that there are some situations where this is not possible, but to the best of your ability, work with the parents to make sure you are offering them the support they need in order for the entire family to heal and grow together.

We have already explored how to set boundaries without shaming or shutting the child's play down. When a parent is in the room, the therapist must be willing to coach the parent on how to set boundaries. This will first involve modeling to the parent how to do so.

When Jordan was 6, his aunt adopted him after his parents were placed in jail for neglect and child abuse. During Jordan's therapy, he explored many of the experiences that he'd had while living with his parents. Initially, his play was incredibly hyper-aroused as he played through feelings of terror, hypervigilance, and lack of safety. Using the methods outlined in this book, I was able to help him learn how to regulate through his dysregulation and eventually integrate the feelings and sensations that he was working through. Once he learned how to connect to himself, his play shifted towards hypo-arousal, as he allowed the sadness and feeling of not being wanted to come into the play. Again I worked with him to help him integrate his feelings. As Jordan's play became more and more regulated, I sensed that it might be time for his aunt to join the sessions. It just so happened that Jordan was feeling the same way, because the next session he asked me if his aunt could come in.

Once in the session, Jordan started to throw things at his aunt in an attempt to set her up to feel and understand what he had gone through. Jordan's aunt looked overwhelmed, which was my cue to start to coach her by modeling first. I walked over to Jordan, looked him in the eyes, and said, "Jordan, it is really important to you that your aunt understands how you felt. Show her another way." As Jordan looked around the room to find another way, I explained to his aunt the importance of setting boundaries this way. Later in the session, Jordan again tried to overwhelm his aunt by pushing a pillow up against her, smothering her. I quickly got right next to his aunt and coached her how to set the boundary so that she could practice doing it. Not only was his aunt able to set the boundary without shaming Jordan, but she was able to understand that his behaviors were his way of helping her understand all of the overwhelm he had experienced inside. She also learned that she could set boundaries with him at home in this way, allowing their relationship to continue to strengthen. She later shared with me that this way of setting boundaries, along with strengthening her ability to become his external regulator, was invaluable to their relationship, and that his need to overwhelm her at home subsided drastically.

In summary, here are some suggestions for when a parent joins the session.

- The parent sits on the floor next to you so that you can support the parent's nervous system regulation.
- You become a coach.
- It is your responsibility to become the external regulator for both the parent and the child until the parent is able to fully take over.

CHAPTER 14 KEY POINTS

- Aggression in the playroom is not only challenging for therapists; it is also challenging for parents. Parents need additional support when they are in the playroom and the child begins to play aggressively.
- Regardless of the play therapy theory you work from, working with parents is an important part of the therapy.
- When the parent is in the play therapy session, it is time to coach.
- In a play therapy session with a parent, the therapist becomes the external regulator for all of the nervous systems in the room—theirs, the child's, and the parent's.
- The therapist must be willing to coach the parent on how to set boundaries so that the parents can stay within their window of tolerance during the session.

FINAL THOUGHTS

Learning how to work with aggression in the playroom is an ongoing journey with yourself and with your clients. It will be filled with moments of attunement and mis-attunement. There will be many moments of rupture and repair. It is not about "getting it right" in the playroom. It is about being real and authentic, with an intention to heal. It is about understanding that everything occurring in your sessions is a shared experience. These shared experiences are the doorway into greater depths of healing and transformation.

Take a deep breath, trust yourself, feel your body, and step inside.

ACKNOWLEDGMENTS

To all my students over the years who kept asking me to write this book—it was your vulnerability with your stories and your belief in me that inspired me to write this book for you.

This book would not have happened without the help of my loved ones, my friends, and the enormous support system that believed in me more than I believed in myself at times. Writing this book required me to face my own fears in order to discover my authentic voice. It also required me to embody all of the teachings that I present in this book. I am so grateful for the transformation that has occurred within me as a result. A special thank-you goes to the following people:

My family, especially my mom, Terri Terni, and my dad, Steve Terni, for your love and deep belief in me.

My daughter, Avery, for your unyielding patience and understanding while I spent hours writing. You are my greatest inspiration.

Jeremy Dion, for cheerleading me on and believing in my potential. Thank you for caring for our daughter and giving me the freedom to pursue my dreams.

My dear friends Enette Pauze, Jolina Karen, and Jayson Gaddis for helping me face my fears when I got stuck writing this book and needed some encouragement.

Kathy Clarke and Khris Rolfe, for your unwavering support and belief in the power of this work. Your belief in me and in Synergetic Play Therapy gives me wings.

My team at the Synergetic Play Therapy Institute for all you do to help me be me.

Dr. John Demartini, for giving me permission to challenge my "shoulds" and for encouraging me to go for it in life.

Lari Magnum, who guides me weekly back to myself, helping me see that the greatest gift I can offer others is presence.

Thank you also to Stephen Terni, my twin brother, for being with me every step of the way.

Krista Reinhardt-Ruprecht, for your artistic talent with the illustrations in this book.

Dave Garrison, this book would not have happened without you. Thank you for holding my hand through the journey of bringing this book to life.

Bonnie Badenoch, for writing the foreword of this book and for the many beautiful conversations about the brain that inspired me beyond words and helped shape the content in this book.

Deborah Malmud and Norton for your patience and guidance as I wrote this book. Your feedback was spot-on every time and invaluable.

My child clients, for swinging swords at me, handcuffing me, shooting me, yelling at me, and working so hard to help me understand your world. This book is also for you.

REFERENCES

Badenoch, B. (2008). *Being a brain-wise therapist: A practical guide to interpersonal neurobiology.* New York, NY: Norton.

Badenoch, B. (2011). *The brain-savvy therapist's workbook.* New York, NY: Norton.

Badenoch, B. (2017). *The heart of trauma.* New York, NY: Norton.

Bandura, A. (1977). *Social learning theory.* Upper Saddle River, NJ: Prentice Hall.

Bratton, S., & Ray, D. (2000). What research shows about play therapy. *International Journal of Play Therapy, 9,* 47–88.

Bratton, S., Ray, D., Rhide, T., & Jones, L. (2005). The efficacy of play therapy with children: A meta-analytic review of treatment outcomes. *Professional Psychology: Research and Practice, 36,* 378–390.

Bullard, D. (2015). Allan Schore on the science of the art of psychotherapy. Retrieved from www.psychotherapy.net/interview/allan-schore-neuroscience-psychotherapy

Bushman, B. (2002). Does venting anger feed or extinguish the flame? *Catharsis, Rumination, Distraction, Anger and Aggressive Responding, 28,* 724–731.

Dales, S., & Jerry, P. (2008). Attachment, affect regulation and mutual synchrony in adult psychotherapy. *American Journal of Psychotherapy, 62(3),* 300.

Demartini, J. (2010). *Inspired destiny.* Carlsbad, CA: Hay House.

Dion, L., & Gray, K. (2014). Impact of therapist authentic expression on emotional tolerance in Synergetic Play Therapy. *International Journal of Play Therapy, 23,* 55–67.

Dispenza, J. (2007). *Evolve your brain: The science of changing your mind.* Deerfield Beach, FL: Health Communications.

Edelman, G. M. (1987). *Neural Darwinism.* New York, NY: Basic Books.

Elbert, T., & Schauer, M. (2010). Dissociation following traumatic stress: Etiology and treatment. *Journal of Psychology, 218(2),* 109–127.

Fonagy, P., & Target, M. (2002). *Affect regulation, mentalization and the development of the self.* New York, NY: Other Press.

Geen, R. G., & Quanty, M. B. (1977). The catharsis of aggression: An evaluation of a hypothesis. In L. Berkowitz (Ed.), *Advances in experimental social psychology* (Vol. 10, pp. 1–37). New York, NY: Academic Press.

Gerhardt, S. (2004). *Why love matters: How affection shapes a baby's brain.* New York, NY: Routledge.

Ginott, H. (1965). *Between parent and child*. New York, NY: Macmillan.

Gottman, J. (1997). *Raising an emotionally intelligent child: The heart of parenting*. New York, NY: Fireside.

Heyes, C. (2009). Evolution, development and intentional control of imitation. *Philosophical Transactions of the Royal Society B, 364*, 2293–2298.

Iacoboni, M. (2007). Face to face: The neural basis for social mirroring and empathy. *Psychiatric Annals, 37*(4), 236–241.

Iacoboni, M. (2008). *Mirroring people: The new science of how we connect with others*. New York, NY: Farrar, Straus and Giroux.

Iyengar, B. K. S. (1979). *Light on yoga: Yoga dipika*. New York, NY: Schocken Books.

Kabat-Zinn, J. (1995). *Wherever you go, there you are: Mindfulness meditation in everyday life*. New York, NY: Hyperion.

Kestly, T. (2014). Presence and play: Why mindfulness matters. *International Journal of Play Therapy, 1*, 14-23.

Kestly, T. (2014). *The interpersonal neurobiology of play: Brain-building interventions for emotional well-being*. New York, NY: Norton.

Levy, A. J. (2011). Neurobiology and the therapeutic action of psychoanalytic play therapy with children. *Clinical Social Work Journal, 39*, 50–60. doi:10.1007/s10615-009-0229-x

Marci, C. D., & Reiss, H. (2005). The clinical relevance of psychophysiology: Support for the psychobiology of empathy and psychodynamic process. *American Journal of Psychotherapy, 259*, 213–226.

Mehrabian, A. (1972). *Nonverbal communication*. Chicago, IL: Aldine-Atherton.

Ogden, P., Minton, K., & Pain, C. (2006). *Trauma and the body: A sensorimotor approach to psychotherapy*. New York, NY: Norton.

Ogden, P., Pain, C., Minton, K., & Fisher, J. (2005). Including the body in mainstream psychotherapy for traumatized individuals. *Psychologist-Psychoanalyst, 25*(4), 19–24.

Osho (1983). *Hsin Hsin Ming: The Book of Nothing*. Tao Publishing.

Oxford Dictionaries. Aggression. Retrieved from https://en.oxforddictionaries.com/definition/aggression

Perry, B. D. (2006). Applying principles of neurodevelopment to clinical work with maltreated and traumatized children: The neurosequential model of therapeutics. In N. B. Webb (Ed.), *Working with traumatized youth in child welfare*. New York, NY: Guilford Press.

PESI (2012). Applications of the Adult Attachment Interview with Daniel Siegel. PESI Publishing and Media.

Porges, S. (2011). *The polyvagal theory: Neurophysiological foundations of emo-*

tions, attachment, communication, and self-regulation. New York, NY: Norton.

Post, B. (2009). *The great behavior breakdown*. Palmyra, VA: Post.

Rizzolatti, G., Fogassi, L., & Gallese, V. (2001). Neurophysiological mechanisms underlying the understanding and imitation of action. *Nature Review Neuroscience, 2*, 660–670.

Schaeffer, C., & Drewes, A. (2012). *The therapeutic powers of play: 20 core agents of change*. Hoboken, NJ: Wiley & Sons.

Schore, A. N. (1994). *Affect regulation and the origin of the self: The neurobiology of emotional development*. New York, NY: Erlbaum.

Schore, A. N. (2003). *Affect regulation and the repair of the self*. New York, NY: Norton.

Schwartz, A., & Maiberger, B. (2018). *EMDR therapy and somatic psychology: Interventions to enhance embodiment in trauma treatment*. New York, NY: Norton.

Siegel, D. J. (1999). *The developing mind: How relationships and the brain interact to shape who we are*. New York, NY: Guilford Press.

Siegel, D. J. (2007). *The mindful brain: Reflection and attunement in the cultivation of well-being*. New York, NY: Norton.

Siegel, D. J. (2010). *The mindful therapist: A clinician's guide to mindsight and neural integration*. New York, NY: Norton, 2010.

Siegel, D. J. (2012). *Pocket guide to interpersonal neurobiology*. New York, NY: Norton.

Siegel, D. J. (2013). *Brainstorm*. New York, NY: Penguin Putnam.

Siegel, D. J., & Bryson, T. P. (2011). *The whole brain child: Revolutionary strategies to nurture your child's developing mind*. New York, NY: Delacorte Press.

Tronick, E. (2007). *The neurobehavioral and social-emotional development of infants and children*. New York, NY: Norton.

Tyson, P. (2002). The challenges of psychoanalytic developmental theory. *Journal of the American Psychoanalytic Association, 50*(1), 19–52.

Van der Kolk, B. (2015). *The body keeps the score*. New York, NY: Penguin Books.

Zahavi, D. (2001). Beyond empathy: Phenomenological approaches to intersubjectivity. *Journal of Conscious Studies, 8*, 151-67.

INDEX